PERSONAL FINANCE FOR K-12 TEACHERS

9 HOMEWORK ASSIGNMENTS TO TAKE CONTROL OF YOUR FUTURE

MICHAEL FRIDGEN

ISBN: 978-0-9968574-8-2
Dreamlly Books: Minneapolis, MN

Disclaimer: In providing information, neither Michael Fridgen nor the publisher is acting as a certified financial planner, certified financial advisor, analyst, economist, CPA, accountant, or lawyer. Neither Michael Fridgen nor the publisher makes any recommendations as to any specific securities or investments. All content is for informational and general purposes only and does not constitute financial, accounting, or legal advice. You should consult your own tax, legal, and financial advisors regarding your particular situation. Neither Michael Fridgen nor the publisher accepts any responsibility for any loss which may arise from accessing or reliance on the information in this book, and to the fullest possible extent permitted by law, we exclude all liability for loss or damages, direct or indirect, arising from the use of the information.

Contents

The Big Half-truth: *Money Isn't Everything*

Education is my family's business. My mom taught first and second grade at the same Minnesota public school for over thirty-five years. She has three children—all of us have master's degrees in education. I'm in the middle.

I didn't grow up in extreme poverty, but I didn't grow up in the middle class, either. It was the 1970s in a small rural Minnesota town. My dad cleaned an office building at night.

We lived on a dirt road and didn't have an automatic washing machine. On Saturdays, my mom washed our clothes (most of which she'd made) in a large green tub that sat on heavy metal legs. The tub had a large white agitator that plugged into an unfinished basement wall. We filled the tub with a green garden hose that was connected to a sink.

It was my job to pass the clothes through the ringer. The ringer, also plugged into the wall, was bolted on the edge of the tub. When it was activated, two metal rollers rotated. I fed the clothes through the gap between the rollers as the excess water was pressed back into the tub. There were many dangers. Small items, such as socks, could easily wrap around the bottom roller. Freeing the socks became an annoying delay in the washing process. Other times, if I wasn't being careful, large items would feed through too quickly, causing the top roller to break from its bracket with a loud bang. And, always, there was the ever-present terror of feeding your own hand through the terrible mouth of the ringer.

In the summer we hung the clothes outside to dry. In the winter we dried them on large wooden racks that were set up throughout the basement. If you were really in a hurry to get something dry, and it was winter, you could lay the item outside until it froze solid. A fact unknown to most people who have electric dryers: frozen clothes dry faster than clothes at room temperature.

But we didn't just wash clothes. My mom rinsed out the used Ziploc bags from our lunches and hung those on the line as well. I was in heaven when I went to college—my dorm had automatic washing machines and dryers.

Before I left for college, I had eaten very few store-bought snacks. My mom had made most of the cookies, bars, and cakes I'd ever had. She even made all of our hotdog and hamburger buns. On our birthdays, we got to have a real treat as we were allowed to pick out a cake at the grocery store. Years later, when we were dating, my husband made a cake for me on my birthday. He thought, as most people do, that a homemade cake would be a heart-felt gesture. It was, but I was disappointed. I could have a homemade cake anytime I wanted. On my birthday, I still only feel special if I can pick out my own grocery store cake with beautiful frosting flowers and an expiration date.

It was in this environment that the Big Half-Truth was born. I was raised on the "money isn't everything" philosophy to the degree that it was a religion. We were taught to focus on what we had and not what we didn't have. We learned to be happy in the same way that Dolly Parton was happy when she wore the coat of many colors that her mother made for her. None of these ideas are bad, and they should be taught to children.

However, if these sentiments had been all we were taught, I might have been financially okay. But we were taught more. We were taught that we were happy *because* we didn't have money. We went way beyond Dolly's coat and went into the realm of *Little House on the Prairie.* In that show, the Ingalls were happier, and just all-around better, simply because they had less money than the Olesens. This is a dangerous sentiment.

Growing up, I truly believed that rich people were bad. They were corrupt and evil. Nobody who had money could possibly be happy behind a smile that was surely fake. Children of wealthy people were not loved and were, most likely, neglected. There was no middle ground in this regard: rich people were crooks.

The worst of the worst, I learned, were those who lived in New York City and worked on Wall Street. They were the people who communed nightly with Satan. They sold their own mothers and probably ate their own babies.

When I look back and examine that time, a hard truth emerges. This "money isn't everything" philosophy was not born of truth. It was a defense mechanism that was born of envy and ignorance.

I, and those like me, had only learned half of the truth. Yes, it might be true that "an apple a day keeps the doctor away." But only if you do a lot of other things to maintain your health (and if you're not allergic to apples). "Better late than never" might be true—unless you miss your flight. "Every cloud has a silver lining," until it's your house that gets destroyed by a tornado. Proverbs are powerful as they guide our thoughts. But they are often half-truths.

Money Isn't Everything, but Everything Requires Money

This is the whole truth: Money isn't everything, but *everything* requires money. As much as Charles Ingalls, in his little prairie house, may have disagreed, we have to recognize that life is better with money. Not only does money provide food, water, and shelter—it also provides safety and security. People who have enough money to support themselves have better relationships. This isn't because money guarantees happiness, but because they don't have the stress of worrying about food, water, shelter, safety, and security.

But above that, money provides education and enlightenment. The internet isn't free, nor is school, nor are books. Everything requires money, and those who have financial security can much more easily attain their dreams. At a base level, in order to get a job, you have to be able to afford a way to get to a job interview. At a higher level, in order to get a job, you have to be able to attain the education and experience necessary for the position.

Money provides experiences and enjoyment. Television, movies, theater, concerts, sports, travel, vacations, picnics, pets, road trips, Christmas, ice cream, children—they all require money.

Teachers and Money

Teachers, more than those in any other profession, ascribe to the half-truth and ignore the whole truth. This is why teachers approach their personal finances in a unique manner. This is also why teachers are easy prey for sketchy financial advisors with false promises.

It's not that teachers are lazy or somehow stupid. It's that the type of people who choose to go into the teaching profession are the type of people who believe in youth. Teachers work each and every day with the future. We all want a future full of noble citizens who have good morals and happy temperaments—teachers are no different. Teachers instill the "money isn't everything" philosophy because they, themselves, want to live in a world where that is true.

However, teaching this half-truth philosophy leads teachers to make reckless and ill-informed decisions when dealing with their own finances. It is certainly why I made terrible financial choices during my eighteen years of public-school teaching. After I became dedicated to learning all I could about finances, it took years to rectify my choices. When it comes to finances, time definitely *is* money. I can never get those lost years (and all that wonderful compound interest) back.

Teachers need to learn, and teach, the whole truth: Money isn't everything, but *everything* requires money.

About This Book

This book contains nine assignments to aid you in your journey as a teacher seeking better financial control. Some of the assignments will require math and research—they are the easy ones. The more difficult assignments will require you to unlearn childhood beliefs. In my own journey, I found that my brain was in no way prepared to handle the unforgiving realism of math until I'd reconciled my psychological barriers. Needless to say, an open mind is required in order to proceed.

It's my hope that upon completing these assignments, you will feel stronger and better prepared to face the future. But even more than that, I hope you will learn that money is not the instrument of the devil. Wealthy people are not all bad. And, it's possible to be financially secure *and* happy.

Assignment Number One: ***Look in the Mirror***

I stated earlier that the "money isn't everything" philosophy is not born of truth. It is a defense mechanism born of envy and ignorance. In this assignment we will tackle all that envy and ignorance.

This will be, by far, the most difficult assignment in this book, because it requires you to admit that you are human. We don't like to do that. We don't like to believe that we are susceptible to the same personality defect that we dislike in others. In my own journey, I was financially paralyzed due to my envy and ignorance. All the money in the world would have been wasted on me had I continued to wallow. Taking a good, long look in the mirror granted me the financial security I have today.

Envy

Let's tackle envy. Have you ever heard any of the following statements in the teachers' lounge?

> *"We are so underpaid."*
>
> *"I could be making so much more money if I quit teaching."*
>
> *"It must be nice to make a lot of money by doing absolutely nothing."*
>
> *"Teachers work harder than any other profession; we should be paid the most."*
>
> *"With my education degree, I could be making more money in the private sector."*

If you answered no, you have never heard any of these statements in the teachers' lounge, then you are lying. I've never been in a teachers' lounge where I haven't heard these statements, usually on a daily basis.

I, myself, was the king of envy. I didn't just say these things, I firmly believed them. I didn't pay any attention to what my current retirement money was doing, because I was too busy complaining about how much money everyone else seemed to have. It was truly a defense mechanism to cover for my faults. As long as I believed the world was against me, I wouldn't have to take accountability for my lack of financial understanding.

Then, my life changed. At thirty-three years old, I got married. My husband worked in a profession that required evening shifts. Since he worked the year around, it made more sense for us to live where he worked—it was a two-hour drive from my school. I already had ten years in at that district, and with a master's degree, I didn't want to leave my years of experience. I spent a year commuting. It was the worst year of my life. Some people love commuting—I hated it. The ten hours every week in my car were draining my soul. In addition, winter in Minnesota can be rough. Two hours of driving is often the difference between blizzard and beautiful. Several times, I was stranded in one place when I needed to be in the other.

I remember listening to talk radio in order to get the road and weather reports. During every commercial break, a man named Dave Lee would go on and on about Perkins Restaurant. I got so tired of listening to him describe pancakes that it made me physically sick. I regret to say that I was not a good teacher that year.

My husband and I decided that I should resign at the end of the school year and look for a new teaching job. However, this was 2007, and the job market in education was not what it is now. I was unable to secure a local teaching job. The baby boomers had already been replaced by the millennials—and they weren't retiring anytime soon. In addition, with a master's degree plus experience, I was expensive.

I searched diligently for other employment. I applied for jobs in business, healthcare, and tourism. I never got so much as a phone interview. Where were all these high-paying jobs that I often said I could get with an education degree? Where were the highly paid opportunities that I frequently stated were waiting for me? It turned out that they weren't real. When I'd inquire nicely about why I wasn't selected for an interview, I was always told that I didn't have the appropriate background. It was almost as if teachers were taboo outside of schools.

Finally, I got a job working in Student Affairs for a small campus of the University of Minnesota. However, my new salary was exactly—to the dollar—$20,000 less than what I'd been making at my public school. And, to add insult to injury, I had to work all year with only twenty-two vacation days. I complained to my husband. His response: "I understand your frustration, but it's hard for me to offer sympathy. This is how the rest of the world operates."

Working summers turned out to not be so bad. Summer in Minnesota is nice and comes without the transportation obstacles of winter. People are generally laid-back and uncharacteristically non-Minnesotan. Working during the summer was actually fun.

But, the days around major holidays soon became a major source of frustration. I was accustomed to automatically getting long breaks for each holiday. Now, if I wanted to go shopping the day after Thanksgiving, I'd have to burn a vacation day. Never in my life had I ever had to use a personal day to see my family. That was my new reality.

When I was teaching, I was on the calendar committee. I remembered arguing over whether December 22 was too close to Christmas to hold classes. Now, I was sitting at my job until 4:30 p.m. on December 24—Christmas Eve. And I had to be back there at 8:00 a.m. on December 26. The same was true for New Year's and the Fourth of July. If I wanted a spring break, I had to use my vacation time. And, that was only if my supervisor approved the request.

One of the hardest things I've ever done is admit to myself that teaching public school was a great gig. The simple truth was this: There is no other job that pays that well and has a schedule as fantastic. I had to admit that all my statements in the teachers' lounge were, indeed, whining out of envy.

Please know that I'm not suggesting teachers stop fighting for better wages. Absolutely, it's important to work for and attain more resources. However, I am suggesting that teachers need to realize how fortunate they are. This, no doubt, is going to make a lot of education blood boil. Many of you will seriously consider burning this book at this point. Please don't. Look in the mirror and try as hard as you can to admit to yourself that around the globe, there are millions of people doing a lot more for a lot less.

The most dangerous thing about envy is that it wastes time. I neglected my personal finances for eighteen years—I believed there was no point in working on them, as American culture was against me. I also had the dangerous, and erroneous, belief that my retirement would somehow magically appear.

The amount of money I wasted during those eighteen years is staggering. It's easy to do the retroactive math, because we know exactly how well various investments performed over those years. I had done serious damage to my life. I needed to realize that it was my fault because I was too stupid to acknowledge that I had been consumed with human envy.

Ignorance

Most people find it difficult to admit to someone else that they don't know something. Teachers find it nearly impossible. This isn't because teachers are inherently flawed. It's because teaching, by its very definition, largely involves knowing what you are talking about. I detested the day that I had to admit to myself that I was ignorant.

Time after time during my teaching tenure, I pretended to know what my local union's financial advisor was talking about. Simply put, I was embarrassed to admit to him that I didn't know even the basic terms of financial literacy. I distinctly remember nodding in agreement when he spoke about basis points—even though I had no idea what they were. (A basis point is one hundredth of one percent. It's primarily used to calculate interest rates and financial commissions.)

I wrote earlier that I moved and eventually left public school teaching because I got married. That's not entirely true. I did have a wedding—at the Mall of America, no less. But we didn't get married on that day, because same-sex marriage wasn't legal yet. However, a few months before the wedding, I went with my future husband to meet with his financial advisor. I'd brought along all my 403(b) statements that I thought were earning me tons of money. The advisor took a long look at them and sighed. He told me that most of my money had gone to commissions and that we'd need time to work it all out. Consequently, I spent the rest of the meeting pretending to know what he and my fiancé were talking about, because I didn't want to seem more stupid than I already did.

Driving back to my apartment that afternoon, I pounded my fist on the steering wheel out of frustration. It was so difficult to realize that I didn't know what I was doing. I was about to buy a house with someone I wasn't legally married to, combine our finances, and possibly change my career. What in the hell was I thinking? How could I, a person with a graduate degree, not know how much money I had?

I had been raised to believe that, because money wasn't everything, I didn't really need to know much about it. But my parents can only claim a small portion of the blame. A larger part of my ignorance belongs to a culture that taught me it was impossible to understand finances. Finance, I thought, was a mysterious entity that belonged to guys in suits who worked on Wall Street. I also thought that the world of finances was too complicated for ordinary people to understand.

However, above all, I had to admit to myself that all this was my own damn fault. I thought about those guys who worked with my school district selling 403(b) products. These were young guys right out of college. What intelligence did they have that I didn't? The reason I didn't understand my own finances wasn't because I was stupid, it was because I was lazy.

I started learning by reading books and listening to podcasts about finances. I took several online university courses in financial literacy. I stopped pretending to know things and actively questioned our financial advisor when I didn't understand something. It was a lot of hard work that had to be accomplished on my own time while I continued to teach and start a life together with my husband.

I made lots of changes and smart choices. By the time we were legally able to get married, five years later, I had enough money to quit my job and start writing full-time. Although, I don't want you to think that there was magic or a rich dead uncle involved. We changed our home, cars, spending patterns, and even the way we ate. That was how our dreams came true.

Looking back, I wouldn't trade that learning process for anything. After ten years of learning all I can, I am strong and confident. I can't express how good it feels to know that, even if we both stopped working, my husband and I will be financially okay until we die.

Everyone can know these things. There is no mysterious and complicated world of Wall Street. But you have to begin by admitting that you are ignorant about finances.

Look in the Mirror

It's often been said that when you cheat at the card game Solitaire, you are only cheating yourself. The same is true about finances. If you cheat in your ability to take a hard look at yourself, then you are only cheating yourself. Don't do it—you work way too hard to cheat on yourself.

Stand up. Look in the mirror and tackle your envy. Get your financial statements and acknowledge your ignorance. Look at them and circle what you don't understand. You wouldn't expect less from your students, so don't expect less from yourself.

Assignment Number Two:
Stay Out of the Teacher's Lounge

Oh, the teacher's lounge—that wonderful desert oasis! That place with the invisible force field that disintegrates anyone without a high school diploma into a mass of blood and flesh! I often laughed in there until my stomach hurt. I cried in there on 9/11.

In this assignment, I'm not suggesting that you literally stay out of the teacher's lounge. It's a great place to connect, rest, and prepare. But I am instructing you to avoid conversations about finances. Especially when those conversations involve boastful colleagues or professional salespeople.

Boastful Colleagues

We've all been there, and we all know *that* person. I'm talking about your colleagues who, even though they make the same money as you, always have a fantastic car. They go on elaborate vacations and live in enormous McMansions next to the "good" elementary school in your town. They always seem to know absolutely everything about wine and, even though everyone else is covered with dry-erase dust, they are perpetually in pristine condition.

Avoid these people at all costs. Yes, it's partly because of envy. But it's also because these people make you feel as if you are doing something wrong. And, most of all, never listen to any financial advice they give.

Remember when I said in the introduction that it's okay to be wealthy? It still is. The problem with these people is that they are not wealthy—they are the fools that are cheating in their own game of Solitaire. None of them have what they boast to have. Don't worry about them. I firmly believe, and even mathematically know, that life will catch up to them.

Even if you are doing something wrong (and who among us isn't?), listening to them boast will not help your situation.

But don't be mean or talk back. Just smile and agree on the outside, while you ignore them on the inside. (This is how most of us Minnesotans get through life anyway.) As hard as you try, you will never be able to change them—and it's really none of your business. Let their boasts slip off you and pool on the floor.

Most of all, never take financial advice from a friend, family member, or colleague. (I'll get to where you should go for financial advice in a bit.) By doing this, you can mess up your finances and your relationships.

As a general rule, financial advice is only good when you have sought it out yourself. Avoid all talk about finances in the teacher's lounge—it simply doesn't belong there.

The Professional Salesperson

I've decided to write this section as a play. Not only have I witnessed this scene on several occasions, but I've been part of it myself. Don't get the idea that this play is entertaining—it should be the most terrifying thing you've read in this book so far.

The Teacher and the Leacher:
a play in one act

CAST

Mr. Fridgen—a teacher in his mid-thirties. Very cute, but envious and ignorant.

Mark Handsome—a financial consultant for the Blackboard Life Insurance Company. He's in his mid-twenties, extremely good-looking, and dressed in a full suit. He has that hair you only see in Lifetime movies and shampoo commercials.

SCENE

It's morning in the teacher's lounge. MARK HANDSOME is sitting next to a large round table. He has placed his briefcase on the table and arranged several piles of brochures next to it. A box of donuts from the expensive bakery in town sits open in the middle of the table. MR. FRIDGEN enters the room with an empty water bottle. He notices the donuts out of the corner of his eye, but heads immediately to the sink to fill his bottle.

Mark: Good morning, how are you?

Mr. Fridgen: I'm fine—thanks.

MARK: Help yourself to a donut if you want. I'm Mark Handsome from BLIC Financial Services.

(Mr. Fridgen smiles and sits down at the table. He read in the principal's bulletin that a financial representative would be in the lounge this morning. His water bottle was just an excuse to get a free donut. He wastes no time in choosing the Long John filled with icing. He loves this particular donut more than life itself.)

MR. FRIDGEN: I'm Michael Fridgen, I'm a teacher here.

MARK: While you eat your donut, can I ask you about your plans for retirement?

MR. FRIDGEN: Yes ... well ... I've actually been working a lot on that lately. I'm considering my options and doing research—that kind of stuff. *(He's clearly lying.)*

MARK: Well, I'm here to talk about your 403(b). Have you started contributing to one yet?

MR. FRIDGEN: Not exactly. I'm still considering what I want to do. *(Still lying. He's spent maybe 2.13 seconds doing any sort of research on it.)*

MARK: As you probably know, your district will match whatever you contribute up to $5,000. If you're not contributing, then you are wasting all that money—right?

MR. FRIDGEN: Yes, I guess I am.

MARK: Okay, we need to take care of that right now. The best thing for you is to open a variable annuity with BLIC Financial Services. We can do the paperwork right here—it will only take a few minutes. I'm sure you know all about the benefits of a variable annuity—but, would you like me to summarize them? Just so that I can offer the best service. *(Mark knows that Fridgen has no clue what a variable annuity is. He's attempting to flatter Fridgen's ego in order to make a sale.)*

MR. FRIDGEN: Sure—go ahead.

MARK: Well, with a variable annuity you'll contribute pre-tax dollars out of every paycheck. That will lower your income so that you'll pay less taxes. Also, the school district will match whatever you put in. But here's the best part of a variable annuity: You can never lose what you put in. That's right—if the account makes money, you get what you put in plus whatever was made. But even if the account loses money, you'll still get what you put in. It's what we in the financial world call a "no-brainer." You can't lose.

MR. FRIDGEN: That actually sounds great. I've been considering a variable annuity for some time. *(Liar!)* I should probably ask, how much it will cost to have you do this for me. How much do you charge on this thing?

MARK: Well, the news just keeps getting better. There is no commission on a variable annuity. I'm paid a salary directly from Blackboard Life Insur—oh, excuse me, I mean BLIC Financial Services. They pay my salary and you don't give me a dime.

MR. FRIDGEN: This all sounds good. Can we do the paperwork?

(It takes just a few minutes to fill out the necessary forms.)

MARK: Okay, that's all I need. I'll go ahead and file these for you with HR—you don't have to do a thing.

MR. FRIDGEN: Great! I have to get to my classroom. Thanks for the donut.

MARK: See-ya, I'll be in touch.

(Mr. Fridgen leaves with his water bottle. Mark Handsome picks up his phone, dials a number, and holds it to his ear.)

MARK: Hi Kurt, it's Mark. Yep, I just signed up a new one—I'll scan the paperwork this morning. Yep—variable annuity—no, of course I didn't tell him that the only way he can get what he put in is to die. What?—no, of course I also didn't tell him that if the account makes money the only way to get all of it out is to die. Yes, he asked about commission—no, he didn't ask where BLIC gets the money to pay me ... Who knows what he thinks? Maybe he assumes you get the money from a tree in order to pay me—as long as he doesn't figure out that BLIC charges a huge fee, then I really don't care. Anyway, Kurt, I have to go—another one is coming in pretending that she doesn't know there are donuts ... Ha! ... Yep—Mr. Fridgen has no idea how much he just paid for that donut.

END SCENE

The amount of unscrupulous sales that occur inside the sacred space of the teachers' lounge is repulsive. No matter what they tell you, the people with the free donuts are not financial consults, financial planners, or anything of the sort. They are salespeople, plain and simple. As a general rule, do not engage in business with people who are way too eager to get the paperwork signed—ever.

I'm also wary of consulting with people outside the teacher's lounge who work specifically with teachers. Most often, these people are employed with agencies that work in partnership with the various levels of teachers unions in the country. Because they work only with teachers, these agencies frequently sponsor union events and staff development. While it's great that they sponsor these things, you must remember that every dollar they spend is a dollar taken from you. Your retirement money is for you and your family's well-being. Let the union sponsor its own events. If you choose to pay for staff development, so be it. But your retirement dollars need to be maximized to work for you and you alone.

Creating a financial plan for your future takes lots of time, lots of effort, and lots of math. It's not something that can be done in fifteen minutes before your students arrive. It's also not something that your union has any business being involved in.

When you begin to investigate agencies that offer financial services, you will find many that focus on niche clients. Financial services for teachers, financial services for Lutherans, financial services for gay people, for women, ... the list goes on and on. Be careful with these types of providers. They are too eager to get your money. Since they focus on something in your life that you are passionate about, they can easily manipulate your emotions. When our emotions are manipulated, all of us are more susceptible to overlooking high fees and low quality.

You wouldn't trust your children or students to someone who just showed up at your door. Why would you do the same with your finances? Don't work with anyone who has found you. Work with people whom you investigate and choose.

How to Move Out of the Teacher's Lounge

First, you need to find a certified financial planner who is not connected to education. You want to be sure that the person you find has the initials CFP after their name—plus, a little R in a circle (®).

When those letters and the registered trademark symbol appear, it means that the person you are working with has passed the CFP Board Exam. This exam is an extremely rigorous test of advanced financial mathematics. Also, anyone who uses the CFP® label has taken an oath to act as a fiduciary. This means that they are legally bound to put your best interests first.

Second, meet with the CFP for a lengthy information-gathering session. The CFP will ask you a lot of questions—seriously, *a lot*. You may feel that the questions are even a bit too personal. But stay with it. A quality CFP needs to know everything about you and your family. You should bring all your financial statements along with you to the meeting. Be prepared to discuss marriages, divorces, births, deaths, homes, cars, insurance, boats, vacations, illnesses, heartbreaks, dreams, and many other things. You want to work with a CFP who charges a one-time fee to create a plan. That fee should be less than $400. You do not want your CFP to also be the person who actually invests your money. That should be a different person who will change a commission fee during an ongoing relationship (we'll discuss this later). For now, the CFP you choose will be someone you are working with on a limited timeframe to create a financial plan. If your life changes and you need a new plan, you can work with the same CFP again (paying another one-time fee) or choose someone else to update your plan.

Third, the CFP will use your information to generate a comprehensive plan for you to follow. The CFP will present this plan to you in person. Everything will be thought about. But be prepared: you may not like what you hear. It's not the CFP's goal to be your friend. Their goal is for you to attain financial stability for the rest of your life. You may be told that you are spending way too much. You may be told that you are woefully unprepared to retire. You may be told to keep driving your current car for ten more years. You may even be told that you need to sell your house. Just remember that the CFP is working to get you where you want to be, and all options are on the table.

You don't *have* to do anything with the CFP's advice. You could simply pay them, take the document, and leave. But you shouldn't. Don't cheat at Solitaire. The sooner you do the difficult work, the sooner you will be able to enjoy the fruits of your labors.

Fourth, the CFP will recommend the investments you should use for your 403(b) funds. (We will learn about these specific investments in assignment four.) Your detailed financial plan will include recommended agencies that will do the actual investing. At this point, your relationship with the CFP should terminate. The CFP has made a plan for you; you do not want that same person to do your investing. Consider the investment options that the CFP recommends, and make a decision.

Fifth, invest your 403(b) funds with an appropriate entity. This will require more than one conversation in the teachers' lounge over a donut. You see, in order for your school district to send pretax dollars from your paycheck, your investment entity needs to be a designated vendor of the school district. It may quite possibly turn out that the entity your CFP recommended is not a designated vendor—but it can be. You will need to be diligent. Contact your district's HR Department and work with them. Many times, the investment entity will help you complete this process. But, be advised: HR Departments are notoriously reluctant to add new vendors. This is because it makes extra work for them. (So, how did Mark Handsome and the others who come to the teacher's lounge get to be designated vendors? Well, it turns out that the folks in HR also like donuts.) You need to always remember that HR is there to work with you. They need to create a path for you to access the benefits that you have earned.

Stay Out of the Teachers' Lounge

I almost shake with revulsion when I think about what I did in the teachers' lounge. I trusted my future, and my financial security, to a guy I'd never met and had only talked with for about ten minutes. Ten minutes! I did this because I was lazy and didn't want to think about it anymore. (And, when I look in the mirror, I hate to admit that I was also taken in by his handsome appearance. Ugh! Sometimes, I dislike being human.) When I finally got my financial act together, it took years, fees, and substantial penalties to fix my mistakes. As Mark Handsome stated, that donut did, indeed, cost me a lot of money.

My advice is to never speak finances in the teachers' lounge. They're way too important and way too personal. However, you should still go in there and grab the free donut—your less-informed colleagues have already paid for them, so you might as well enjoy. Just smile, thank the salesperson, and politely state that you are not interested.

Assignment Number Three: *Investigate and Monitor Your Teacher Retirement System*

Ignorance is bliss. Has there ever been a truer statement uttered? I long for the days when I drifted through life believing that, when I retired, I'd get a nice pension check every month until I died. My mom, who retired in 2003, was doing it. Why should it be any different for me?

Well, it is different—very different. Let's start by learning how public teachers' pensions have evolved. All pensions are considered a Defined Benefit Plan, meaning you are supposed to get a specific and consistent benefit.

The current school system in America is a product of post-World War Two prosperity. At that time, it was common for the employees of any company to receive the promise of a pension when they retired—school districts were no different. Local school districts created pensions for the teachers who retired after a specific number of years in that district. The district was setting aside money for this to occur.

But it became apparent in the 1970s that local school districts were unable to create and manage the funds necessary to provide for large groups of people until they died. Consequently, states began to merge local school pension plans into one large plan that was controlled by the state legislature. These are the Teacher Retirement Systems (TRS) that we have today. In Minnesota, it's called the Minnesota Teachers Retirement Association. In your state, the name will be different. Whatever the name, they are your TRS. (Some of the larger city districts still control their own funds—we'll get to those in a bit.)

Teachers Retirement Systems (TRS)

The concept was originally quite sound. From every paycheck you get, a pre-determined percent of your salary is automatically sent to your TRS. Your school district also sends a percent of your salary. This pre-determined percent will vary depending upon which state you live in. Some of the states do not permit public employees to contribute to federal social security. In these states, the percent sent to the TRS is higher. About 40 percent of teachers work in states that do not participate in federal social security. Regardless of which type of state you work in, participation in the TRS is mandatory.

The TRS takes your money, plus your district's contribution, and uses it to pay for the salaries and buildings of the TRS. Then, the bulk of the funds is invested. This large amount of money grows and grows. After a pre-determined amount of time, you will become vested. This means that when you reach the pre-determined retirement age, you will get a check every month until you die. The longer you teach after you're vested, the more money you will get in your retirement check.

For example, in Minnesota, you are vested after three years of service in a Minnesota school district. If you never teach again, you will still receive a check each month when you reach retirement age. But that check will be very, very small. Again, the longer you teach, the more you will receive back.

At some point, you will reach the retirement age. This age is set by the TRS and in most cases it requires legislative approval. The baby boomers retired under something called the "rule of 90." This meant that when their age plus their years of teaching equaled 90, they could retire and receive a full TRS check. Your TRS check will be determined using a formula set by the TRS. The formula will be a percent of the average salary you earned in, usually, your highest five years of income. (Some places, and the federal government, still utilize a high-three formula.) The percent of your average salary will differ depending upon your state. Those who live in the states where teachers do not participate in social security get a higher percent. You can also decide, when you retire, to accept a slightly lower amount in your check so that your spouse can continue to receive the funds if you should die first. This is called a survivorship.

That's how the system is supposed to work. And it did work for quite some time. However, there is an inherent problem in the model. The employees of the TRS don't really have an incentive to maintain a quality fund, because they know they won't be around when you finally decide to retire. This leads these funds to become heavily invested in stock speculation and other risky ventures. Today, there are enormous problems with most of the state systems that need to be addressed.

Problems Arise

In the early 2000s, the TRS plans still controlled by large city districts started to become financially insolvent. Most of these plans had to be legislatively absorbed into the larger state plans. For example, in 2006, the Minneapolis Teachers Retirement Fund Association was absorbed by the Minnesota Teachers Retirement Association because they were headed for financial disaster. Combining city plans with large state plans was supposed to make a stronger overall plan. It didn't really work out that way.

Today, even the large state systems are beginning to fail. In 2017, the Hechinger Report found that the Colorado TRS was $29 *billion* dollars short of being able to provide for retirees. That's *billion*—with a B. Colorado is not alone. In Alaska, the TRS was dissolved all together. It moved from being a defined benefit plan to a defined contribution plan. This eliminated the state TRS's responsibility to provide a guaranteed check to retirees. Consequently, in Alaska, there is no such thing as a teacher's pension any longer. Imagine if this happens to you when you're sixty years old.

Most teachers assume that if their TRS fails, then the state will have to bail them out. I wish that were true. In 2020, the Atlanta Journal-Constitution reported that, if the state were to bail out their TRS, Georgia would need to contribute $2.4 billion each year starting in 2025. By 2045, only twenty years later, Georgia would need to come up with $4.4 billion ever year. This would make it, at that time, the largest expenditure of the state's budget. Paying for retired teachers would cost the state of Georgia more than it pays for current teachers, road construction, health services, and all other state agencies. So, in Georgia, the question will not be: *Should we bail out the retired teachers?* The questions will be: *Is it mathematically possible to bail out the retired teachers?*

But don't lose all hope just yet. There are some things you can do to help ensure that your TRS will be there for you.

You Can Fix It

First, you can hope for the best but prepare for the worst. Hopefully, you will get a check from your TRS until you die. However, if you don't, you need to start planning now. By becoming financially stable without counting on a TRS check, you can alleviate the stress of worrying about your TRS. The rest of the assignments in this book will start you on this journey.

Second, you need to investigate and monitor your TRS. Each of these systems is run by a board that consists of people appointed by the legislature and people elected by the teachers themselves. (I'm willing to bet that you've received ballots for these TRS positions and have quickly thrown them away.) These elected people have a tremendous amount of power over your future finances. Find out who they are. Contact them. Contact them often.

There are four ways that a TRS can work to become more financially solvent.

1. Reduce internal TRS cost.
2. Raise the current retirement age.
3. Raise the percent of contributions current employees make.
4. Reduce benefits from current retirees.

Among these options, only number one is fairly painless. Contact your TRS board and discover how much it costs the organization to maintain itself. Put pressure on them to reduce building and travel expenses. I was astounded, for example, when I found out the amount of money the Minnesota Teachers Retirement Association spends on board member travel.

Options two through four are terrible. Who, in their right mind, would want to work longer, contribute more, and receive less? Well, because you are educated, you do. If options two through four were implemented now, even at a low level, it would make your later retirement much better. Simply put: If we don't raise the retirement age to sixty-nine now, then the state will be forced to raise it to seventy-five later. Or, think about it like this: Would you rather contribute 5 percent more of your salary now, or lose 50 percent of your TRS check later? Whatever you are hesitant to do now will be done to you later—it's pretty much a mathematical fact.

You, and all other teachers, have got to start taking control of the TRS empire in this country. You may be beginning to realize a hard truth in this book: A small amount of bitter medicine now will provide for a cure much later. But it's so hard to take that medicine!

According to the Atlanta Journal-Constitution, in early 2020 the Georgia House of Representatives proposed a bill that would require two things. First, current retirees would receive only one cost-of-living increase each year instead of two. Second, current teachers would no longer be able to count unused sick leave toward their pension. But the bill went nowhere because, according to the House Retirement Committee, they were "flooded with emails."

Someone had to organize the email campaign against TRS reform in Georgia. Whoever did that certainly does not understand basic financial math. But I somehow have the feeling that they won't be around when the system fails for future retirees. Another problem of the TRS model: those with the power have less years ahead, and consequently, a lot less to lose.

There is no easy way to complete this assignment. There is no cheat sheet or open-book test on this one. You have two tasks:

1. Stabilize your financial plan so that you don't have to rely on a TRS check.
2. Bug the crap out of your TRS board until they implement sound financial decisions that raise the retirement age, raise employee contribution, and lower retiree benefits.

You won't win any awards for doing this work. You will probably be hated by the people who don't understand. Just keep the big picture—the future—in mind. You don't want to raise the retirement age, contribute more, and receive less because you're mean. You want to do these things so that all teachers can retire comfortably and be rewarded for their hard work.

First Recess Break:
The Continuing Saga of Ebenezer Scrooge

I love Charles Dickens's *A Christmas Carol*. It's about as perfect a story as there could be. It has it all: drama, romance, comedy, mysterious characters, charming children, turmoil, and lots of heartfelt emotion. It's also a story about business and finances. The older I get, and the more financially literate I become, the more sympathetic Scrooge appears. Here's what may, or may not, have happened after Scrooge brought Christmas to the Cratchits.

The Continuing Saga of Ebenezer Scrooge

And so, as Tiny Tim observed, God bless Us, Every One!

Scrooge was delighted and relieved. He was delighted that he finally understood what everyone had been so happy about all this time. He was relieved that he had not, indeed, died as was foretold by the horrible Spirit of Christmases Yet to Come.

"Al right, all 'a 'ye!" shouted Mrs. Cratchit. "It's pas' time fer 'ye all to get out so's the children can get off ta bed!"

Scrooge, after having just experienced his first joyful Christmas, was now about to experience his first anti-climactic Christmas Night. The Cratchit children ran off at their mother's command. Tiny Tim quickly hopped after them as he forgot his little wooden crutch among the gifts that Scrooge had brought.

"Well, Mr. Scrooge," said Bob Cratchit. "As my wife said, it's now time for us to settle down. I will see you at the office tomorrow. And, thank you, for the most wonderful Christmas dinner, all the gifts, and my new raise."

"No, my dear Bob," replied Scrooge with a slight bow, "thank you."

He threw on his coat, grabbed his hat, kissed Mrs. Cratchit goodbye (much to her horror) and walked out into the cold London air. He breathed deeply and set off toward his home. Along the way, he passed other Londoners who were heading to their homes after various Christmas festivities. They looked tired.

When he approached his door, he took a second look at his door knocker, just to make sure that it was, indeed, a door knocker and not the face of Jacob Marley. Again, he breathed deeply as he noticed the brass lion staring back at him and not the image of an old man with a bandage tied around his head.

Once he was inside there was no need for him to change into his nightshirt. He'd been running around London in it all day like the jolliest fool this side of the Thames. He took off his coat and flung it onto the floor, along with his top hat. He ran up the stairs, put on his nightcap, and jumped into his bed.

Despite the fact that he hadn't gotten much sleep the night before, Scrooge had another restless night. He fell in and out of several dreams that involved the Spirits of Christmases Past and Christmas Present. However, as the night progressed, he found that the ghostly and grim image of the Spirit of Christmases Yet to Come appeared more frequently in his dreams. Toward morning, he awoke screaming at what was a nightmare featuring the cloaked specter.

Scrooge felt odd, as if he'd drunk way too much wassail the night before. Perhaps he had—he couldn't actually remember. He dressed slowly, stumbled down his stairs, and walked directly to his office without putting on his coat and top hat.

As soon as he arrived inside his office, he placed one piece of coal in the stove and lit the fire. Then, he remembered that he had reformed and scooped an entire shovel full of coal through the warming iron door.

He was alone and it was quiet. Bob Cratchit had not yet arrived. He was surprised to acknowledge that he felt a bit disappointed. He wondered why there weren't people in his office, helping him to celebrate his reformation. He briefly attempted to recover the spirit of Christmas in his heart; however, his heart didn't feel as Christmassy on the 26th as it had on the 25th.

Suddenly, the outside door to the office opened.

"Ah, 'ello Mr. Scrooge," said a rather tall woman as she entered through the door. She was wearing a new coat. On her head sat a rather smart looking hat with an enormous blue plume coming out of the top. Scrooge recognized her as a woman he had made a mortgage to some years earlier.

"Yes, hello," Scrooge replied. "Please come in, Missus ... ah ..."

"Missus Primrose Copperbutt is me name," the woman replied. "You 'old the mortgage on me 'ouse."

"Yes, I remember. What can I do for you this fine day?"

"Ah, I can see that ya really 'ave changed! It's jus' as me neighbors told me. Well, I come to ask about me neighbors, in fact. See, yesterday, ya went an' told me neighbors that their loan to ya was forgiven. Ya said that they could 'ave their place free an' clear."

"Yes, well, in fact, I did do that," said Scrooge. "I had evicted them on Christmas Eve and, since I've had a change of heart, I wanted to rectify the situation."

"An' that's why I come. See, I know that me neighbors, nice as they are, 'ave missed a good many payments to ya. I know that me neighbors owe money all over London. Well, I come to ask if I can be forgiven on me own loan. See, I 'ave never missed a payment to ya. If ya is willing to forgive me neighbors that 'ave stiffed ya time and time again, then ya are surely goin' to forgive a soul such as mine that 'as never been bad to ya."

"Ah, well," stammered Scrooge, "I hadn't really had a chance to think about it yet. I suppose that what you say makes sense. And it does seem fair to forgive your loan if I was willing to forgive theirs. But, you see, if I—"

"Oh, thank ya, thank ya!" interrupted Primrose Copperbutt. "I jus' knew ya was a changed man! Now, me 'ome is all me own an I don't owe a cent more!"

She squealed with delight as she quickly turned and left the office before Scrooge had a chance to say anything else. Scrooge sat down at his desk, a bit bewildered.

"I really should have thought this through," Scrooge said out loud as he put his head into his hands. "It feels so good to help people. I loved seeing how excited Primrose Copperbutt was. However, can I forgive any other mortgages? Can I forgive any other loan? Surely Copperbutt will tell all of her neighbors. I will go broke if I forgive them all. I'll lose my business. I'll lose my home. Bob Cratchit will be out of a job. I won't be able to pay Tiny Tim's medical bills. My housekeeper will have to become a prostitute, even though she's seen many decades and is missing a leg. And what about my nephew, Fred? He has put up with my angry mood all these years. He and his wife deserve to get a great many gold coins from me. Now, he will go to debtors' prison and his wife will also have to be a prostitute. Hopefully she will fare better at that task than my housekeeper.

"Perhaps I went too far in my reformation. I learned from the Spirits that money is nothing. But, then, I learned from Primrose Copperbutt that I do need money to do all the good things I want to do. I must find a way to live somewhere between."

Scrooge stood up and walked over to a mirror that was attached to the wall above the stove. He looked at his face with an expression of resolve.

"Yes," said Scrooge, "that's what I'll do. I will find a way to protect my assets first, and then go forward and do good things. I'm certain that the Sprits will approve."

He smiled into the mirror as the softly falling snow fell gently past the window and onto a glistening London street.

THE END

Assignment Number Four: *Discover Where Your 403(b) Funds Are Invested*

Because of the degradation of pensions, severances, and other types of defined benefit plans, the 403(b) has become the most important retirement device for teachers to understand. A fundamental change in philosophy, from employers holding retirement responsibility to employees holding retirement responsibility, increased the importance of the 403(b) by astronomical proportions. There is nothing you can do about the change in philosophy—that ship has sailed. But you can maximize the amazing potential of being able to steer your own ship.

A 403(b) is a defined contribution plan. This means that your employer has defined the amount of contributions they make on your behalf while you are working. Contrast this to a defined benefit plan where the employer defines what benefit you will get when you retire.

There are three main types of defined contribution plans in the United States. They all act pretty much the same. A 403(b) is for people who work for a public entity, such as a school district. A 401(k) is for people who work in the private sector. If you know someone who works for the federal government, their plan is called a TSP. (TSP stands for Thrift Savings Plan. But don't let the name fool you—there is nothing thrifty about it. TSP is the gold standard of defined contribution plans.)

Your employer will dictate how much money you are able to contribute from each of your paychecks into your 403(b). Then, your employer will match that amount up to a limit that has also been pre-determined. Usually, the amount you can contribute will increase with years of service. If you work for a public school, and are unionized, the amounts of you and your district's contributions are negotiated as part of your contract. It's important for union negotiators to understand that increasing the district's match is most often worth more than increasing actual salaries.

Once your employer sends the funds to your chosen 403(b) vendor, they are free and clear of it—that's the whole point. Employers (school districts) have moved the responsibility for your retirement entirely to you. They no longer have to worry if they have enough money to pay for all their retirees.

Yes, once the money has been contributed, it's completely up to you to decide where it goes. Although, here is where problems can arise.

Where, exactly, is your 403(b)?

I once met a teacher who had been contributing to his 403(b) for twelve years. Of course, his school district had been matching his contribution for the entire time. I asked him how his 403(b) funds were invested. He replied, "Well, they are in the 403(b)." That's not an answer. A 403(b) is just a set of rules and nothing more. When we investigated, it turned out that all his 403(b) money—over the course of twelve years—had been invested in cash. He was earning practically nothing! Those who had invested their 403(b) money in an index fund for those twelve years had earned between 10-12%.

The Grocery Store Metaphor

In order to really understand what all this means, we are going to compare the defined contribution plan to a grocery store. We'll use this metaphor for the rest of this book.

Imagine that you are shopping at a grocery store. You've entered the store and grabbed a shopping cart. However, you are a very organized shopper. You don't like to just throw things into your cart. Instead, you organize as you shop. So, before you enter the store, you place several baskets into your cart.

Each of these baskets has a pre-determined purpose. One of the baskets is for frozen foods only. Another is for meats. A third basket is for foods that need time to be prepared before you can enjoy them. A fourth basket is for snacks that can be enjoyed immediately—they are delicious, but not that good for you. A fifth basket is for food that you don't want to eat until a specific event arises, such as Christmas or Thanksgiving. You can put any number of baskets into your shopping cart, each with its own set of rules.

Finally, you enter the grocery store and proceed through the aisles. You select items and put them in the appropriate baskets. You realize that if you put ice cream into the snack basket, back at home it may end up in the pantry instead of the freezer. Your ice cream will be ruined and you won't be able to enjoy it. So, you are quite careful that each item goes in the correct basket.

Because you are so organized, when you get home it doesn't take a lot of effort to put your groceries where they belong. Then, you can sit and relax. You can enjoy your food by following the rules of when it can be prepared and eaten.

In this metaphor, you have three things in your control: the shopping cart, the baskets, and the items themselves. Now, let's talk about how each of these impacts your financial future.

Your Shopping Cart

The purpose of a shopping cart is to hold things and make it easier for you to facilitate the act of buying groceries. Shopping carts normally have the name of the grocery store written on the side. The shopping cart is your portfolio. It's a collection of investments you hold that are facilitated by a third party.

The third party is whoever you choose. It's usually a broker, a bank, a discount brokerage firm, a non-profit financial service, or (if you took the free donut) an insurance company. You will need to investigate to discover which shopping cart is right for you. But, be advised, some grocery stores charge you to use their shopping carts.

Insurance is a necessary evil of life (we'll cover that in assignment seven). But insurance companies charge a lot to use their shopping carts. So do traditional brokers. It should not come as a surprise that banks like to hold onto their money and their cart fees reflect that. Non-profit financial services use a portion of your contributions to support their cause. Giving to charity is great—but do it on your own and not as part of your retirement shopping cart.

A discount brokerage firm is probably the best shopping cart for your 403(b) baskets. The name is a bit misleading—they don't offer products that are discounted or somehow inferior. Before 1976, all financial transactions were standardized by the federal government and assigned fees. In 1976, these transactions were deregulated. Consequently, firms were born that would invest money with lower, or discounted, fees. They became known as discount brokerage firms. Charles Schwab, TD Ameritrade, Fidelity, and E*Trade are examples of discount brokerage firms.

But it's up to you to investigate and make the choice that's right for you. Find out how much they charge for their services (their shopping cart) and move forward. At this point, you may have to work with your district's HR Department if the shopping cart you choose is not already a designated vendor in your school district.

Your Baskets

The purpose of a basket is to hold items that will be used according to a pre-determined set of rules. Each basket comes with advantages and disadvantages. And, not all baskets are created equal. Some are insulated and made of metal—these cost more to use. Others are made of cheap plastic—but they serve their purpose well and carry groceries just the same. Following is a list of the most common baskets and some of the characteristics they contain.

403(b)

This is the basket we've been talking about for this entire assignment. Here is where you, and your district, will deposit the pre-tax funds you have earned. Remember, just having the money in the basket will do absolutely nothing until you purchase some items—we'll get to that soon. In the meantime, your money will grow until you are at least 59.5 years old. Then, you can withdraw from the fund, pay the appropriate taxes, and enjoy your life. If you make any early withdrawals, you will have to pay a penalty. There are limits to what you can contribute, and your district will only match up to an amount specified in your teaching contract.

Roth 403(b)

You can do a little happy dance if your district has approved a vendor that offers a Roth 403(b). If not, work with your HR to try to get one. A Roth is a special type of 403(b) that offers an amazing benefit. For a regular 403(b), you contribute money before it is taxed (this way you get more in your immediate paycheck). But, for a Roth 403(b), you contribute money *after* you have paid ordinary income tax on it. This money is then matched by your district and put into the basket. After you are 59.5 years old, you can withdraw the fund. Here is where the magic of the Roth pays-off: any money you take from a Roth 403(b) is free of tax. That's right! If you have $100,000 in your Roth 403(b) you get to actually have all $100,000. You are sacrificing a little bit of money from your current paycheck to get a lot of money later on.

Again, there are limits to the amount you can contribute and penalties for early withdraws. You need to seriously consider opening a Roth 403(b) if it's an option for you. It might be the best gift you give yourself.

IRA

IRA stands for Individual Retirement Plan. Even if you are married, it will belong only to you. An IRA acts a lot like a 403(b), except that your district will not add anything to whatever you contribute. You will pay taxes when you want to withdraw the money sometime after age 59.5. There are penalties for using your money early.

Roth IRA

A Roth IRA acts like a Roth 403(b) without your school district matching your contribution. But, again, the magic is in the tax benefits. You will pay tax on the money you contribute now; however, when you use the money later in life, you get to use *all* the money—tax-free. There are limits to what you can contribute and penalties for early withdraws. Do not overlook this basket.

A note about the 403(b) versus the IRA. You always want to fund a 403(b) basket *before* you fund anything else. This is because your district will match your contribution to a 403(b). Don't let this free money pass you by. IRAs are for *after* you've maxed-out your contributions to a 403(b), or for people who work for districts that don't provide a 403(b).

Investment Accounts

Regular investments accounts are for people who have completely maxed-out all their contributions to defined retirement plans. Another way to say it: Having the problem of not being able to contribute anything more to a retirement plan is a great problem to have. It means that you have extra funds and are planning for your future instead of buying a new car.

Opening an investment account is the least desirable of the retirement options, but it's better than keeping your money in your sock drawer. For these accounts, you will contribute money that you've already paid taxes on. But, unlike with a Roth, you will pay taxes on any of the gains you make. For example, let's assume you put $10,000 in an investment account, and ten years later, when you take out all the money, it is worth $11,000. You will need to pay taxes on the $1,000 and subtract that amount from the $11,000. (There are ways to off-set that tax burden by selling items in your basket at a loss, but that's a topic for another book.)

ESAs and 529 Plans

The last of the most common types of baskets that teachers tend to use are accounts meant to raise funds for future college expenses. ESA stands for Education Savings Account; the 529 plan is a type of ESA. Mostly, these are plans that parents open to save for their children's education. There are a lot of rules to follow if you want to contribute to this type of basket.

If you are interested in opening one of these accounts, please seriously consider paying a Certified Financial Advisor (CFP®) before you proceed. There are many pros and many cons to consider. Sometimes, saving in one of these plans can actually make college cost more for your children. You need to be careful in this realm. A CFP can use your goals, plus their advanced skills in financial mathematics, to compute your options.

Also, saving for your child's education should come *after* you've fully funded your own retirement. Yes, giving your child a college education could be an amazing gift. Everyone wants to send their kid out into the world without debt. However, as selfish as it sounds, you must consider your own future first. No kid wants to become an adult who has to deal with parents who are broke.

Of course, there are hundreds of other baskets you might encounter. I've listed by far the most common. Each basket comes with its own set of rules—and its own set of fees. But, the main thing to remember is that the basket does absolutely nothing with just money in it. You must purchase some items with your money.

Items for Your Baskets

While there may be hundreds of baskets for you to choose at the grocery store, there are thousands, even millions, of items available to put in your baskets. When you were choosing baskets, you needed to be concerned about the rules. When you choose items, you must be primarily concerned about the risk. Each item comes with a certain amount of risk—this is where futures are made and lost. Here is where you must not do anything you don't understand, where you must not let anyone talk you into something you are uncomfortable with, and where you must take control of your money.

Following are the most common items that you will encounter. Shop wisely.

Stocks

The stock market is not the evil entity that Hollywood wants you to believe. The United States Stock Exchange has two main purposes: to transfer money through time and space, and to determine the value of items.

Corporations need money in order to do business, maintain their assets, create new products, and accomplish all the other necessary tasks they need. Even if they have cash on hand, which they are most likely saving for a rainy day, corporations want to borrow money from you and me. They do this through the use of securities called stocks and bonds. We'll talk about stocks now and save bonds for just a little later.

When you give money to a corporation so that they can use it, you are actually buying a piece of that company. The company gives you stock as a symbol of what you own. If you buy one share of Disney, you own a very, very—VERY—small part of everything Disney owns. (Yes, you can say that you own part of Disneyland!)

You could go to Charles Schwab (your shopping cart,) put money in an IRA (your basket), and fill it full of Disney stock (your items). At Charles Schwab, you can buy individual stocks for absolutely zero fees. However, putting all your eggs in one basket is extremely risky. What happens if, for whatever reason, Disney makes poor decisions and the company fails? More likely, what happens if an outside and uncontrollable force ruins what Disney owns? Even Disney, as huge as it is, suffered drastically from the 2020 COVID-19 outbreak.

We'll talk more about diversifying later. For now, know that trading in individual stocks can be a risky business. Only do this if you are confident and have extra money that won't ruin your retirement if you lose it. Sometimes, trading in individual stocks can be no better than going to the casino—especially if you are constantly trading and not holding on to stocks for a long period of time.

You may have heard stories about people who speculated on the market and won. Speculators attempt to foresee the future by discerning which companies will do better than others. These are the people who bought large amounts of Amazon stock when it was just a small online bookseller. Good for them! They managed to gain a lot of money, mostly through luck. Any number of online retailers could have been Amazon. And, for some reason, we never hear the stories of those who bought large amounts of stock in companies that failed.

When you own stock, you will experience gains and losses. Hopefully, you will experience larger gains than you do losses—the longer you invest, the better your chances. In the end, you will have money in your basket that has been generated from your stocks. How do you collect the money, and do you pay taxes on it? Well, you need to remember that the basket determines the rules, not the items in it. If you put your money into a Roth basket, and bought stock with it, then you can withdraw your funds after you've reached the age of 59.5 and pay absolutely nothing in taxes. If you put your stocks into an investment account, you can take the money out whenever you want. But you will pay taxes on the gains you have made.

Mutual Funds

The most popular item that people put in their baskets is the mutual fund. This does not, necessarily, mean they are the best option for you. Like everything else, you need to investigate and be especially concerned about fees with this item.

A mutual fund is a collection of stocks that is controlled by a fund manager. When you buy a mutual fund, you are spreading your risk across any number of stocks.

Let's say that a fund manager chooses 100 corporations that they think will gain in value. They will buy a certain amount of stock of each of those 100 corporations. Then, they will break their whole collection (their mutual fund) into shares. In this example, let's suppose that the fund manager broke the collection into 1,000 equal pieces. When you buy a share of this mutual fund, you are buying 1/1,000 of the amount of stock the manager purchased from each of the 100 corporations.

Mutual funds can go up and down depending upon how the individual corporations in the fund are faring. The fund manager has an immense amount of power, and can buy and sell stocks within the fund. Essentially, they are buying and selling on your behalf. When they buy stock in Company XYZ, so have you.

The great benefit of mutual funds is that they automatically spread your risk as they diversify your basket for you. This is why so many people buy them. The negatives are that you must pay a fee to the fund manager, and you are at their whim.

Again, how you access any money earned in a mutual fund will depend upon which basket you put it in.

ETFs

An Exchange-Traded Fund (ETF) is a special kind of mutual fund. The New York Stock Exchange is open every business day from 9:30 a.m. to 4:00 p.m. Eastern Time. During that entire period, stocks and bonds are constantly bought and sold. If a mutual fund is a collection of items, then it stands to reason that the value of any mutual fund changes constantly during the trading day. You will never know *exactly* what your share of a mutual fund is worth, because each of the individual stocks in the fund must be calculated at the *exact* moment you want to know. This is why shares in mutual funds can only be bought and sold at the conclusion of the trading day.

Enter the ETF—a device born of modern technology. An ETF, using computers, *can* calculate the *exact* value of your share of a mutual fund at the *exact* moment you want to know. If you own an ETF, you can buy and sell your shares during the trading day. This can be a huge advantage for people with the expertise and time to monitor the markets closely.

But, just like with regular mutual funds, each ETF has a manager that charges a fee. However, unlike regular mutual funds, an ETF manager has the added power of being able to make quick decisions—they don't have to wait for the stock exchange to close in order to make changes. This power can be good or bad. Some ETF managers may miss opportunities because they are trigger-happy, while others stay in poor-performing stocks because they are too complacent.

Index Funds

In order to understand index funds, you must first understand the stock market index. How do we know how well the stock exchange is doing at any particular time? When people go around stating that the market is up or down, how do they know that? There are billions of transactions that occur each day around the world. The tool we use to discover whether the general trend is up or down is the stock market index.

An index is the average value of a pre-determined collection of corporations at a specific point in time. While there are hundreds of indexes, in the United States we normally focus on the three most popular.

The Dow Jones Industrial Average, named after its creators Charles Dow and Edward Jones in 1896, is a collection of thirty corporations. By quickly looking at the average value of these thirty stocks, we can get a fairly good idea of how the market is doing. But, if Disney is part of it, and Walt didn't even go to California until 1923, how can it be part of an 1896 index? Well, the Dow Jones changes its list of corporations from time to time as companies fail, merge, and appear on the market. Coca-Cola was added in 1932 and remains in the index today. In 2018, Walgreens replaced General Electric.

The Standard and Poor's 500, or S&P 500, is a collection of the 500 largest publicly traded companies in the United States. Companies are added and removed to keep the index current. The third popular index, the NASDAQ Composite Index, is a collection of almost 3,000 corporations. Because 50 percent of the NASDAQ is always in technology-related companies, this index is a good indication of where the modern market may be heading.

The item that you may put in your basket is the index fund. An index fund is exactly what it sounds like—it's a mutual fund that contains every stock from a specific index. A Dow Jones Index Fund will contain equal stocks of each of the thirty companies represented by the Dow Jones Industrial Average. If the companies within the Dow Jones change, so will the make-up of the index fund.

Because index funds do not require a fund manager, they normally have lower fees associated with them. Charles Schwab offers an S&P 500 Index Fund for a commission fee of just .02% (or two basis points.) This means that you can go to Charles Schwab and get a shopping cart for free, open a Roth IRA basket for free, and fill it with an S&P 500 Index Fund with a .02% commission. This is a great way to spread out your risk without paying much in fees.

Historically, index funds have out-performed most managed mutual funds. But in order to make money in an index fund, you need to be in the market for the long haul. If you have thirty years ahead of you before you need the money, you need to seriously consider index funds.

Bonds

A bond is just another name for a loan. When a company issues a bond, they are borrowing money from you for a specific period of time. In return for using your money, the company will then pay you a pre-determined amount of interest. In this case, you are not buying a piece of the company as you are with a stock. When you lend money to a company in return for some interest, you are buying a corporate bond. However, there are other types of bonds.

A special kind of bond, the municipal bond, is issued by public entities such as towns, parks, and school districts. In these cases, the public entity asks the voters if it's okay for them to issue bonds. The entity will use the money they collect for whatever purpose they committed to, and the taxpayers will ensure that those who purchased the bonds get their money back, plus interest.

Because bonds act under a pre-determined contract, they carry less risk than stocks. While it does happen that a company or municipality may default on their bonds, it is less probable than a company losing value in their stock. To put it another way, bonds have a contract behind them that guarantees a benefit, while stocks do not.

Here's where bonds start to get a little messy: bonds can be traded at the bond market. The value of a bond is connected to its interest rate and the stability of whatever entity will eventually be responsible for fulfilling the contract. Anything that has value can be traded, and anything that can be traded can go up and down.

For example, let's say that the Dollyville School District wants to build a new high school and issues bonds with taxpayer approval. You buy one of them. Then, for whatever reason, the stock market crashes. Suddenly, your bond looks better for investors because it has more of a guarantee associated with it than the stock market does. Someone, via the bond market, may offer to buy your bond and give you more money than you paid for it. They aren't going to give you what you'd get if you held on to it, because they want that money. But you might be willing to sell it to get some money now that you can do other things with. Conversely, perhaps something happens in Dollyville and the school district might have problems collecting property taxes in the future. Now, your bond is risky. Someone, via the bond market, may offer to buy your bond for less than you paid for it. But, at least you'd be getting something. So, you sell it. Now, all Dollyville bonds will be worth less because the sellers, via the market, have determined their lower value.

Typically, the bond market is safer than the stock market. But that doesn't mean that there is no risk at all. Market volatility can, and does, impact the bond market. Even more than that, the prevailing interest rate set by the United States Federal Reserve can raise and lower the bond market in extremely short periods of time.

You need to be careful if someone is trying to talk you into buying bonds. Don't do anything you don't understand. Because people have the general idea that bonds are safe, they don't take the time to discover which exact types of bonds they are buying.

Municipal bonds are safe because the likelihood that the taxpayers will default on the bond is low. But you might be pressured into buying a bond issued by another country. A Samurai Bond comes from Japan, Panda Bonds are from China, Bulldog Bonds are issued in the United Kingdom, and Maple Bonds derive from Canada. (Each international bond as a unique name. If you live outside the U.S., bonds that originate here are called Yankee Bonds.) Be careful if someone suggests a bond that you don't understand.

Another thing to watch out for are fees. Most bonds have their fees built into them. (In our example, the cost of Dollyville to manage their bonds is considered as part of the bonds themselves—the secretary who is doing the paperwork has already been paid.) You should not have to pay any fees associated with purchasing a bond.

Bond Mutual Funds

Just like a stock market mutual fund, a bond mutual fund is a collection of bonds. Using these, you can spread your risk over many bonds. While the bonds inside the fund will not have a fee, the manager of the bond fund may charge a fee.

Again, just like with stocks, what you can do with the money in a bond fund will depend upon which basket you put it in.

Lifecycle Funds

Lifecycle funds are collections of items that are managed for you over a long period of time. These can be a great choice for someone who doesn't want to be that involved in the short-term management of their money. They will come with the associated fees of managing a fund for such a long time, but the fees may be worth it for the peace of mind.

A lifecycle fund will be managed for a specific period of time. If you are looking at retiring in thirty years, you can purchase a fund that expires in thirty years. Then, you sit back while the manager(s) adjust the fund as time goes on. In the beginning of the fund, they will invest in risky items. You will have lots of time to recover if any of these items fail. But, as the expiration date approaches, they will remove risky investments and replace them with safer items.

The name of the fund is usually written as the year it will be fully realized. For example, a 2030 lifecycle fund will gain its full potential in the year 2030.

Variable Annuities

There are some books on personal finances that don't mention insurance-based investments at all. This is because they are not always seen as worthy investments. The authors of books that neglect to mention them understand that insurance is for asset protection, not for investing. However, I have to mention them here because, for whatever reason, insurance salespeople love to target teachers. Maybe I should ask the question differently: What is it about teachers that makes them susceptible to these high-cost products? It could be that teachers are often strapped for time or that teachers are too supportive by nature—it's probably a combination of both.

The most popular insurance-based investment that you are likely to encounter is the variable annuity. This is an investment that is tied to a portfolio of underlying mutual funds. It's sort of like you are owning a few mutual funds through a third person. Depending upon the performance of the underlying funds, the variable annuity rises and falls in value. When you reach a pre-determined age set by the annuity company, you arrange with them to receive payments based upon the amount of money you have accumulated. Sounds good, right?

Well, variable annuities are not all they're cracked up to be. The salesperson will be sure to sell you on the fact that you can never lose what you put in. Even if the underlying funds fall, the insurance company will guarantee that you get back what you put in.

However, what they don't like to point out is that in order for you to get that amount of money, you have to die.

I don't know about you, but ten dollars given to me while I'm alive is worth more than one million dollars given to me while I'm dead. Of course, my estate could inherit the money. But saving for retirement is meant to provide for me when I'm old and want to relax—saving for retirement is not meant to be a device to save money for my heirs. If you've already fully funded your retirement, and you have extra money that you know you will have no use for, then a variable annuity might be something you could consider with your heirs in mind.

The largest disadvantage with variable annuities is the extensive schedule of fees. They are expensive to buy and maintain. Also, these investments come with stiff penalties when you want to withdraw your money.

Money Market

All this talk of risk might scare you. It's perfectly fine to be apprehensive about investing—after all, it's possible to lose everything you have. Maybe investing in anything that comes with a risk is just not for you. There are some quite wealthy people who have never purchased a stock. But, if this is you, remember to still do something with any matching dollars your school district provides. Don't throw away the free money that your district is giving you. At your discount brokerage firm (your shopping cart), you could open a 403(b) (your basket) and fill it with funds in a money market account (your item).

The money market is, basically, a mutual fund of items that are coming to term in the near future. The risk of investment is quite low because the terms of the underlying obligations are so short that it's highly unlikely they will fail.

The low risk of the money market comes with accompanying low yields. This can be a way to earn more interest than a savings account and to acquire your district's matching funds without the risk of investing in other products. Do not feel bad if you take this path. It's not worth it to put your retirement in a higher-yield account if you're going to worry about it every single day.

Other Weird Stuff

There are thousands of other things that you could use in your basket. Speculators, hedge funds, and various investment schemes are always around. Do not do any of this weird stuff unless: A) you have a lot of money that you don't ever need, and B) you really, really, really understand everything about the investment you are buying. This is where entire retirements are lost overnight. Yes, the payouts could be enormous, but they probably won't be. If someone has won the "weird stuff" game, it's really no different than if they'd gone to the casino and hit it big.

Those are the most common shopping carts, baskets, and items that you are likely to encounter on your journey to fully funding your retirement. Before we leave this lengthy assignment, I have just two more things that you need to consider.

Fees, Fees, and Fees

Each shopping cart, basket, and item can come with a fee. Many people run around concerned about taxes. However, in my opinion, fees are worse and hardly ever talked about. The reason why I believe fees are worse than taxes is because you are paying them early, and throughout, the investment period. This is all money that will be missing from your basket—meaning, this is all money that will never earn compound interest for you. I can't stress enough how important compound interest is for building wealth. Every single cent that you've given to someone else is gone forever and cannot multiply in any way.

Be concerned about fees. When you ask about fees and commissions, don't let anyone tell you something that you don't understand. Ask them to explain exactly what they mean. If you have to, ask them to explain using hypothetical numbers. Often, they will use basis points to explain a fee in hopes that you don't know what basis points are and you are too afraid to ask. A basis point is 1/100 of a percent. If someone is charging 75 basis points, that's .75%—way too much for most financial products.

Diversify, Diversify, and Diversify

Your best chance for success lies in your money's ability to withstand any number of market circumstances. If you put all your eggs in one basket, you could end up with a bunch of lovely chickens that make more eggs—or you could end up with a bunch of broken eggs.

Strive for a variety of items. This is where a Certified Financial Planner (CFP®) can be of great assistance. That person can recommend an allocation based on where you are now and where you want to be.

When you are young and at the beginning of your career, you can fill all your baskets with riskier items because you will have time to recover after they fall (which will always happen.) As you age, you will need to change your allocations so that your entire shopping cart carries less risk. A diversified shopping cart will not look the same for everyone.

You've maybe seen those people on television who lost everything to Bernie Madoff or some other crook. This would not have happened to those people if they had just given Bernie one egg and put the others somewhere else.

Finally, the Assignment

And now, finally, it's time for you to work on assignment number four. It's going to take time and lots of effort. Find out exactly where all your money is located. Make a chart and draw out all your shopping carts, baskets, and items. If you don't have any yet, then this is the time to start.

Seek professional advice if you need to. Don't do anything you don't understand. Ask lots of questions before you proceed. Be concerned about fees and make sure you diversify.

It's a lot of work. But your sixty-year-old self will be extremely grateful. Just think about all those seventy-five-year-old teachers working on lesson plans while you are relaxing somewhere.

Assignment Number Five: *Confront and Eliminate Debt*

Before we start this assignment, there are two things you should know about me. First, I absolutely love theme parks. Second, I used to be morbidly obese. (It's interesting to note that when my finances were a mess, my body was also a mess. But that's a discussion for a whole different type of book.)

In the summer of 2003, I was at Valleyfair, our regional theme park just outside of the Twin Cities. It was a glorious day in Minnesota. Summer in Minnesota beats the weather anyplace else on Earth—it's only that summer in Minnesota is short and lasts for about six days in the middle of July. Anyway, the sun was shining, the sky was crystal blue, and a light breeze was coming down from Canada. It was perfect.

I went for my first ride of the season on my favorite roller coaster. That was when my perfect day came to an abrupt halt. The lap bar wouldn't close because my stomach was in the way. As hard as the attendant tried, it just wasn't going to work. Consequently, I had to perform the dreaded walk of shame. I had to saunter past all the people waiting in line. They tried not to look at me, but they couldn't help themselves—they were all looking at me and pretending not to know why I'd been kicked off the ride. But they weren't fooling me. They all knew. How could they not?

I was devastated. It was 50% embarrassing, 40% humiliating, and 10% humorous. I guess that was when I, a hard-core sugar addict, hit rock bottom.

At first, I tried to lose weight with magic. This means that I didn't really change anything and just hoped that, somehow, the fitness fairy would appear and wave a wand while I was sitting on the couch with a bowl of homemade cookie dough. The fairy's magic would allow me to stuff my face and lose the pounds. But alas, there is no fitness fairy. Then, I tried every gimmick advertised on daytime television. None of that worked either. Next, I switched to all kinds of foods made with artificial fats and sweeteners. All that did was make me bigger and gassy.

In order to lose weight, I had to go on a diet. It's about as close to hell as is possible on this planet. I had to write down absolutely everything I ate and drank. Restricting the amount of calories in my diet was the only thing that worked. Eventually, and slowly, I lost 110 pounds.

It feels so good to be healthy, as the benefits are outstanding. My whole life changed. Why hadn't I done it sooner? Because it was very, very difficult—that's why. And, like most humans, I despise having even one moment of discomfort. Conquering debt is exactly like being on a diet. The only way to do it is to write down every cent you spend and slowly chip away at the problem.

Debt

There are thousands of books about personal finances and even more blogs, vlogs, podcasts, and television shows. The pundits of these various outlets might disagree about the specifics of reaching financial stability—that's why it's important for you to do your research. However, there are some themes on which almost all financial experts agree. One of them is debt elimination.

Debt is a monster. All that wonderful compound interest—the gift of mathematics that makes your baskets grow—works against you when you have debt. Debt turns your credit card bill into a car, your car into a house, and your house into a lifetime of earnings.

Just like with dieting, there is only one way to tackle debt. There is no magical debt fairy. You must pay it down, and the only way to do that is to watch every single cent you spend. It's tedious, boring, frustrating, and sometimes embarrassing. But take it from me, being free of all debt feels as good as losing a hundred pounds. No, that's wrong—it feels better!

In order for you to enjoy a full retirement, you must retire with absolutely no debt. There is no wiggle room in this regard. The faster you eliminate debt, the more money you will be able to save. Let's talk about the four most common types of debt that teachers have: student loans, mortgages, car loans, and consumer debt. One of them you won't be able to do much about, but the other three are completely under your control.

Student Loans

This is the debt that you, unfortunately, won't be able to do much about, except pay it off. One of the problems with student loans is that you accumulate them when you are too young to really understand what you are doing. You can't sell the product they provided for you in exchange for a cheaper model. You can't invite someone else to share in the debt. You can't even get the debt discharged in bankruptcy. There are only two ways to get out of student debt: pay it off or die.

Please don't get into the thinking that the United States will someday eliminate student debt. It is never going to happen. It has nothing to do with politicians, voters, banks, taxes, or the colleges themselves—it has everything to do with mathematics. There will never be enough money to cancel student debt. I've met some people that have stopped paying their student loans because they believe that the government will erase their debt when the right person is elected. They are only making their situation worse by wrecking their credit score. In turn, a low credit score will make most other bills in their lives more expensive. Again, this promise sounds great coming from politicians, but math shows us its nearly impossible.

The only option you really have is to pay it off. It's going to be difficult. It might be the most difficult thing you'll ever do. Every single cent you spend on something you don't absolutely need is a cent that you could have paid toward your student loans. If you have student loans, then you cannot go to a coffee shop. You also can't go on vacation or buy alcohol. You can't give to any charity. You can't have a big wedding. If you have student debt, they only thing you can do is use every cent to pay it off. Yes, it's terrible. You might feel that it's really, really unfair. You will scream and cry over it. Just know that the faster you pay it off, the faster you can go on vacation.

I can hear the whining coming from future readers as I type this portion of the book. The sound is so loud it seeps through the keys of my computer and wraps itself around my throat. One sentiment is the loudest: *Why even bother having a college degree if I can't enjoy my life?* Well, here is the hard truth: you signed on the dotted line. Some people graduated from high school and started working as janitors. These people have been scrubbing other people's shitty toilets while you were partying in your dorm. Now, about the time that you're finally getting your degree, these janitors are debt free and being promoted to manager. Everyone has to pay the piper, and now it's your turn.

Mortgages

Unlike student debt, there is something you can do about home debt. You can manage it, change it, and even eliminate it. Also, when you are ready for a mortgage, you are older and more educated about debt.

Before we started to take control of our finances, my husband and I lived in a 3,200 square foot home on a half-acre of land. We both said that we loved the house and needed all the space in order to live and be safe. We were kidding ourselves—we really wanted that house because we had a childish need to show off to others.

Do not fall into the trap of buying more house than you need. We sold that place and moved into a 925-square-foot home. We are happier in our cozy home than we ever were rambling around that house.

You must get over the feeling that others are judging you by your house. Does your cousin live in a mansion? Does your best friend from high school live on a cul-de-sac in the best part of town? Does the paraprofessional in your classroom have a pool? Be happy for them! Go and swim in the pool.

Yes, real estate can be an investment. But real estate is different than any other investment because it takes a lot of money to maintain it. Plus, you have to live somewhere. When you sell your investment you have to buy another one, unless you move into someone else's basement. In addition, nobody takes out a loan so that they can buy a Roth IRA, but people do that for houses every single day. A house, as an investment, is not a guarantee of anything.

Real estate comes with lots of costs. All of these costs will be subtracted from any eventual financial return. When considering real estate, you must remember property taxes, homeowners insurance, yard care, new roofs, new furnaces, new appliances, remodeling that horrible, outdated bathroom, and all the other expenses associated with owning a home. People who buy huge homes in order to be impressive have even more expenses because they have more of everything. And, everyone seems to fill their homes with stuff—regardless the size. The larger the home you have, the more money you will waste on stuff.

I'm a fan of renting. When you sit down and run all the numbers, you will find that, in the end, renting and buying are about even. This is because the cost of home ownership is very high when you consider all the extra expenses that renters don't have. Don't get into the trap of thinking that renting is throwing away your money. Take the money you would have spent on a down payment and invest it. Take the money you would be spending on appliances, yard care, property taxes, insurance, and upkeep—invest that money, too. At the end of the day, you will have spent (and earned) an equal amount of money. The decision to rent or buy is a lifestyle choice, not a financial one.

If you do decide to purchase a house, you must have a 20% down payment. If you can't come up with 20%—then, unfortunately, you cannot buy that house. You'll have to either look for something cheaper or save more money. People who don't have 20% down must purchase mortgage insurance. This insurance is required to cover any loss of equity the mortgage company would assume if you can't pay your mortgage, for whatever reason, early in the life of your purchase. It's a completely needless product because you can avoid it entirely by having a 20% down payment. Mortgage insurance really is flushing your money down the toilet each month.

Mortgages are debt. Every cent of interest you give the mortgage company is a cent that you can't earn compound interest on. It's in your best interest to pay off your home as soon as possible. The easiest way to do this is to be careful of what you buy. You have a lot of control with this type of debt.

Car Loans

Cars are similar to homes. They are so easy to overbuy because they are a supposed immediate sign of your prosperity. But if you aren't careful, your car will become so similar to a home that you will end up living in one.

My husband and I live eight blocks from my mother-in-law. We each used to have our own car. Now, the three of us share a baseline Toyota Prius with cloth seats. We've been doing this for eight years and it's never been as annoying as I had initially feared. When I am inconvenienced because I don't have access to the car, I sit down with my financial calculator and compute the amount we've saved on maintenance, insurance, and license fees all these years. Then, I take into account the initial purchase price of the car we never bought. That money has been sitting in an index fund compounding itself.

Buy a used car that you can afford. Don't worry about what your cousin drives. Try, as hard as you can, to buy a car with cash. If you must finance it, then go for a loan no longer than thirty-six months. If you can't find a car that you can afford with a thirty-six-month loan, then you are looking at too much car for you. Every cent you spend on a car loan is one less cent that will work for you.

While I'm a fan of renting, I am not a fan of leasing. Imagine that you are renting an apartment and the roof starts to leak. What would you do if the landlord charged you for a new roof? You'd file a report with the attorney general! What would you do if the leasing office said you could only live in your apartment for twenty days each month? You'd tell those people to go screw themselves. When you lease a vehicle, unlike renting an apartment, you are responsible for the maintenance and repair. Most leases will only allow you to drive 12,000 miles each year. (Who in the United States drives only 12,000 miles each year?) The reason why people choose to lease a car, instead of buying, is that they can get a much more expensive car for a cheaper payment. Don't fall into this trap. Buy a car you can afford.

The best way to stop feeling like you are being judged by your car is to stop doing the same to everyone else. When you drive down the highway, don't assume that the woman next to you in the 2005 base model with 150,000 miles is a drug addict. She's probably the smartest person on the road. Likewise, that guy who just passed you in the brand-new SUV is eating ramen noodles for every meal because he has no money.

Consumer Debt

This is the easiest form of debt to avoid. You might not be able to avoid a mortgage because you have to live somewhere. You may have to hold a loan against your vehicle because you need to be able to get to work. But nobody needs consumer debt.

When it comes to consumer debt, you must act like an adult. There is no reason to ever carry a balance on any credit card. Use credit cards as a way to pay for things you need and can afford. Do not use credit cards as credit.

Because I'm a theme park junkie, I charge everything to my Chase Disney Visa. It has a picture of Mickey Mouse on it. I pay it off, in full, every single month. I have never—ever—paid even one cent of interest or fees on this card. Depending upon what I purchase, I get 1-2% back in Disney Dollars. Since I always pay the full bill, these reward dollars are completely free money for me. On all our many trips to Disneyland or Walt Disney World, my husband and I have never spent a cent on food. We use my Disney Dollars for all of it. (You might wonder how we afford to go to these expensive resorts multiple times each year. Well, it's because we've followed all the advice in this book!)

Credit card interest is completely insane. I guess Chase and Disney have to get my reward dollars from somewhere—and they're getting it from people who carry a balance. You don't need to pay for my food at Cinderella's Royal Table.

Don't ever charge anything that you can't pay at the end of the month. Yes, again, it's not much fun. If credit cards are really a problem for you, consider getting a debit card so that it's impossible to overspend. (Well, you can deplete your debit card. But your stomach will, eventually, force you to prioritize your spending.)

This is what I want you to do. When you are shopping and are tempted to charge something that you don't need, and don't have the money for, just think about me. Think about me sitting at the Magic Kingdom and stuffing my face with a Mickey Mouse-shaped pretzel. Do you really want what you are about to buy? Do you really want to pay for my pretzel?

Excuses, Excuses, Excuses

In order to tackle debt, you must face your excuses. Yes, it will be extremely difficult. But stand in front of the mirror and acknowledge that you are human. Acknowledge that you make excuses. Have you ever said, or felt, one of these sentiments?

- I have to live in a big house in a new neighborhood in order to stay safe.
- I have to drive a car that costs more than $30,000 in order to stay safe.
- My kids deserve a happy childhood in a big house.
- I deserve to go on a vacation I can't afford. I worked hard for it.
- I need to buy a piece of jewelry because I've been depressed lately.
- I love to eat at trendy restaurants because I get so much enjoyment from it.
- If I can't enjoy my life, then why bother working?
- If I don't go out and spend money with my friends, then I won't have any friends.
- My kids need a lot of stuff or they won't fit in—and that will hurt them for life.

It's hard to acknowledge our excuses because we don't like to be reminded of this very human personality defect. To complicate matters, advertisers know that you make these excuses, and they use them to their benefit. So do car dealers, real estate agents, jewelry store clerks, travel agents, restaurant owners, and everyone that sells stuff for kids.

Yes, of course, we all want to be safe in our homes and cars. But you don't have to spend a fortune in order to accomplish this. Make sensible choices based on your finances and not rash decisions based on television commercials.

You probably do need a vacation—especially if you're a teacher. But if you can't afford one, then you simply can't afford one. It's not fair. It's reality.

Most likely, the most difficult human emotion to confront is the desire for your kids to have more than you had. This desire has ruined the personal finances of teachers for decades. If there is any one truth in the universe, it's this: an ounce of prevention today is worth a pound of cure tomorrow. It might be rough for your kids now, but they will thank you greatly when you are secure in your retirement. When I was growing up, I had to spend Saturday morning feeding clothes through a ringer. Now, I get to spend *every* morning doing exactly what I want. Would my life be different if I'd had lots of things as a kid? Absolutely—and I shudder to think how bad things could have turned out. As my Grandma Francy often said, "If your kids don't cry when they're young, then you will cry when they're old."

Don't fall into the excuse that you must spend money in order to enjoy life and have friends. Tell your friends what you can and cannot afford. The real ones will stick around. There are so many things you can do to have fun that cost nothing at all. Get used to saying, "I can't afford it," today. Then, when you are retired in a nice home and can comfortably deal with emergencies plus go on vacation, you can listen to your friends as they scream, "I can't afford it!"

Assignment Number Six: ***Save, Save, and Save Some More***

Saving is related to tackling debt because the only way to do it is to eliminate spending. However, it's so much more enjoyable, because you can actually see the benefit instead of letting it go to some banker somewhere. I don't make many guarantees in this book. That's because it's a book on finances, and there are no guarantees in that realm. But I will make one absolute guarantee here: The more you save, the more you will enjoy saving, and the less you will spend. In other words, the hardest dollar to save is the first one. Each dollar after that gets easier and easier until you love seeing how much you can save each month.

In order to consider how much money we are really saving, we have to consider the true cost of things we buy. Every single thing we buy, from the cheapest candy to a home, has a true cost that is higher than the purchase price. This is because you could have invested the money you spent. Although, this does not mean that you shouldn't ever buy anything. You'd starve and be awfully cold at night! It does mean, however, that you need to seriously consider the true cost of things you want and don't need.

To do this, you need to combine a lot of critical thinking with a little math. Thinking about true cost is like thinking about true crime—you need to be a detective and look at your purchases from multiple angles. Let's look at some scenarios as examples.

[Note: For the following scenarios, we are going to assume that the market will have an average rate of return of 7% over the next forty years. In the bull market running up to the year 2020, people had been getting ten years of returns around 10-12%. That's not a normal situation, and those who stake their future on that kind of return will be disappointed. While 7% is still on the optimistic side of things, I chose this number because the average predicted rate of return that teachers retirement systems are currently using is 7.56%. I want to be close to this figure so that you can compare growth. Also, all calculations for this exercise were made on an HP12c Platinum Financial Calculator.]

Jane's Coffee

Jane just graduated from college with a degree in elementary education. Each day at college, she visited the campus coffee shop and purchased a drink that cost four dollars. She is now going to start her first teaching job. She will teach for forty years before she retires.

On her way to school the first day, Jane decides that she will kick the coffee habit. Instead, she takes the twenty dollars each week that she would have spent on coffee and puts it in an index fund (her item) inside of a Roth IRA (her basket) at TD Ameritrade (her shopping cart). However, she only does this for the first year. For the other thirty-nine years, she buys her coffee each day and lets the Roth IRA sit.

On the day she retires, Jane's coffee account is worth $15,573.44. That's a pretty good chunk of money just for giving up one year's worth of coffee.

In order to consider how important time is, let's say that Jane did drink coffee every day for thirty-nine years. Then, during her last year, she deposited the money. In this case, on her retirement day, her coffee fund is worth $1,112.80. This means that giving up coffee in the first year allowed her to make $14,460.64 by doing absolutely nothing.

But what is the true cost of Jane's coffee if she has one every day? It's more than the four-dollar cost multiplied by the business days of her career. She could have been compounding her early missed coffees over the course of forty years. If Jane would have never gone back to coffee, and put that money in her Roth IRA, on her retirement day she would have $210,724.26. That's the true cost of Jane's daily coffee. Also, because that money was in a Roth IRA basket, she gets to use all of it and not spend a cent on taxes.

Jake's Vehicle

Jake is just starting out as a special education teacher. In college, he used his grandma's old car to get around. But now that he's working and has a paycheck, he wants to buy his first real vehicle.

Jake finds a sensible used car, in good shape, for $14,673.25. It's a newer used car with all the modern safety features including a back-up camera and blind spot monitor. It would be exactly what he needs to get around. But then Jake sees the brand-new SUV that he's always wanted. It's loaded with leather seats, seat warmers, and large beverage cups. The SUV costs $42,613.56. He knows it's an extravagance, but the salesperson talks him into it, stating that the SUV is much safer to drive. What is the true cost of Jake's decision?

Well, it's not $42,613.56. Jake needed a car anyway, so we have to compute the amount that he overspent, not the amount he spent. The amount he overspent is $27,940.31. This is derived by subtracting what would have been good enough from the amount he paid. But it's not the true cost of his decision.

Jake had to finance the car. Because he's not had a chance to establish a good credit score yet, Jake's loan is at 6.8%. He makes $500 payments on the loan. Using math, we can determine that he will spend $5,751.43 on interest for the amount he overspent ($27,940.31).

When we add the overspent amount to the interest, we get $33,691.74. But that's still not the true cost of Jake's decision.

If Jake had gone with the sensible car, making payments of $500 each month, he would have paid off the car in 32 months. However, since Jake went with the SUV, he needs 67 months to pay off the vehicle. This means, if he'd purchased the sensible car, made the payments, and then invested the extra $500 each month until he reached the amount of the overspend, then let it sit—on the day he retired in forty years, he would have an extra $180,728.58.

Now, because Jake spent the overspent money, and he also didn't have that money to invest, the true cost of his decision is the overspent amount, plus the interest on that amount, plus what he lost by not having that money to invest. Jake's decision cost him $214,420.32. (Also, when he retired, that SUV was long gone. Jake didn't even remember it. And, to add insult to injury, I'm not even considering the extra fuel that the SUV required.)

Hunter and Emma's Christmas

Hunter and Emma are married teachers. He teaches fourth grade and she's the high school librarian. They have three kids; the oldest is six years old. They are both in their tenth year of teaching.

Emma and Hunter have not done well with their money. Both of them went to private colleges. (Because they are teachers, they are making *exactly* the same salary as teachers who went to state schools. But that's beside the point.) After ten years, Emma still owes $53,000 on her student loans and Hunter owes $29,000 on his. Because they want their kids to have the best childhood possible, they mortgaged a 3,800-square-foot home in the most expensive neighborhood. They each drive SUVs that aren't paid for, and Hunter recently got a great deal on a 2019 Mustang convertible that he uses in the summer.

The couple hasn't saved anything for retirement. They live paycheck to paycheck. Even though their district offers a 403(b) match, they have never participated because they don't have any extra money each month to contribute.

But now it's Christmas. The couple wants to give their kids the best Christmas ever, and they want their family to experience the joy of loving a dog. They purchase a puppy from the cousin of a colleague for $250. The puppy will grow to be a large dog of mixed breeding. The children are delighted, and their Christmas is magical. What is the true cost of the dog?

It's sometimes difficult to predict the true cost of something that can vary. We don't know exactly how much food the dog will eat, how long its lifespan will be, or if the dog will need medical care. In these cases, you will need to use expert advice to predict costs in a rational manner.

The ASPCA sets the first-year cost of owning a dog at $1,843. This includes all the initial supplies, food, grooming, and usual medical needs for one year. Most of these expenses will only occur during the first year. After that, the ASPCA projects that the annual cost of raising a large dog is $875. However, this annual expense does not include any medical needs. An emergency can cost between $3,000 and $5,000. The ASPCA recommends budgeting $250 per year for medical expenses.

Also not included in the annual expenses are any kennel costs when the family goes on vacation. Since they are a family of two teachers, they like to travel during the summer. Even though they take the dog along on most trips, they still spend $300 each year on kennel costs. Finally, the ASPCA recommends planning that a large dog will live for twelve years. We are also going to assume that the dog never has an emergency, nor does it bite anyone. (Both those instances can end up costing a lot.)

The total cost of the first year for this dog is $2,093 (the recommended first-year cost plus the purchase price). The cost for each year after that is $1,425 (the recommended annual cost plus kenneling and medical expenses). Since we know that Hunter and Emma have not contributed a cent to retirement, and have allowed their matching funds to go down the toilet, we must charge them for the entire true cost of the dog. If their future was secure, we could be a little more forgiving.

Taking into account compounding, their thirty years until retirement, and the dog's life expectancy of twelve years, we need three amounts to complete our computation:

A. The total amount of the first year of expenses compounded for thirty years (the time they have until retirement).
B. An annual contribution of $1,425 for eleven years. (Because the dog is already one year old when this begins, we subtract one from twelve.)
C. The total sum of B, compounded for eighteen years (the amount of time between the dog's expected death and the parents' retirement).

The true cost of the dog is A plus C. (We don't need B here, because it is already included in C.) Hunter and Emma will end up paying $97,274.04 for their kids' Christmas present.

Pets are great. There is no doubt that families can experience immense joy in loving pets. However, similar to a vacation, the question is simple: can they afford it? In this case, the answer is a resounding no. Any benefit the children would receive from caring for a dog will be overshadowed by the enormous stress of having parents who are unprepared for the future. This stress, like an IRA, is going to compound. Teenagers are expensive. The huge home is going to need maintenance and renovation. The cars will get old. Emma and Hunter will get old. The bills will keep coming.

The family needs to sell the Mustang and move into a smaller home. If they do that, fund their 403(b), and pay off their student loans, then they can think about getting a dog.

This example is, perhaps, the saddest of them all, because it involves another living thing. If you purchase a car that you cannot afford, at least the car can't feel pain and stress.

Carla's Vacation

Carla is an art teacher in her twelfth year of teaching. She hasn't done well with money, but really wants that to change. She's been watching her spending and has contributed to a 403(b) for the past two years. She recently opened a Roth IRA with her tax return.

Carla's friends from college want her to join them on a cruise over spring break. The total cost of the cruise, with airfare and extra expenses, is $3,567.89. Carla doesn't have that much money to spend because she is concentrating on fully funding her retirement. She tells one of her friends that she just doesn't have the money. However, that friend won't let it go and keeps telling Carla about all the fun she is going to miss. Carla can't resist, and she decides to go.

While on the cruise, Carla has a really good time—at first. She gets an upgraded wine package for $219.99 and goes to the spa with her friends. After the first three days, because she's trying to get on the right financial track, Carla stops at the desk and asks about her current bill. She's owes the ship $614.78 at this time. Carla is devastated. She has the money to pay for it, but she can't stop thinking about how much this trip will cost her retirement.

Carla looks at her friends and sees them ignorantly spending away. She wishes she could be like them. She yearns for those days when she was a blissful spender. However, she can't go back to that time—she's too educated now.

Carla spends the rest of the cruise avoiding extra charges. It makes her annoyed to see her friends doing all these fun and expensive things while she sits on a lounge chair. They even start to tease her and call her "Scrooge McDuck." She gets more annoyed and lashes out at them. Carla avoids the dining room and spends the rest of the cruise in her cabin. What is the true cost of Carla's cruise?

This one is easy, because it doesn't involve math. Sure, the money she spent on the trip could have been compounding for the twenty-eight years she has left of teaching. However, we have to recognize that Carla has already begun to fully fund her retirement. The money she spent on the trip will hurt—but just a little. In this case, the true cost of Carla's vacation was her friendships.

Carla should have followed her instincts and declined the trip. She wasn't feeling secure enough in her finances to enjoy them. Sure, her friends should have been more understanding and appreciated Carla's desire to be financially secure. But, in the end, Carla didn't listen to herself.

Marge's Graduate Degree

Marge is a physical education teacher in a Baltimore suburb. She's in her fifth year of teaching and expects to retire in thirty-five years. She recently began to investigate graduate schools in her area.

Marge already owes $28,456 on her undergraduate student loans. The master's degree she likes best will cost $16,500. She plans to take out student loans for the graduate degree. If she does go back to school, her undergraduate loans can be deferred until she finishes her graduate degree—she plans to take this course. Her interest on her new loans will be 4.53%.

In Marge's school district, teachers with a master's degree make an average of $5,000 more per year, when considering the same step level, as teachers without graduate degrees. Is it in Marge's best interest to get her master's degree?

We don't even need a calculator for this one. She has to pay her undergraduate loans no matter what she does. In order for her master's degree to pay off, she needs to earn back more money than $16,500 plus interest. Making $5,000 extra each year, she should be able to do this in just over four years—she has thirty-three! (We are assuming that Marge can finish her graduate degree in two years.) In case you are interested, if Marge invests her raise of $5,000 at the beginning of each year in an index fund, she will have $633,243.48 when she retires.

However, I would highly encourage Marge to keep paying on her undergraduate loans while she attends graduate school. She won't miss this money, because she's already making these payments each month. The amount of interest she will need to add to her loan, if she defers her undergraduate student loans for two years, is $3,090.

Also, I stated the amount that Marge would have if she invested her $5,000 at the *beginning* of each year. Does it matter if it's at the beginning or end of the year? Yes, it does. When you deposit money at the beginning of a term, you get to earn interest on the money during the first term. That interest compounds itself for the duration of the account. If Marge makes her payment at the end of the year, she will have $594,667.13 when she retires—$38,576.35 less because she waited a year.

Mark's Engagement Ring

Mark is in his eighth year teaching History at Dollyville Senior High School. He's not great with money, but does contribute to his district's 403(b) in order to get the matching funds. He's been dating Jason for over a year, and the two of them have decided to get married. Jason has some expensive tastes and he has been hinting at a $5,000 diamond-and-onyx ring he saw at an upscale jewelry store.

Mark really wants to get that ring for Jason. He doesn't have much in savings. Mark decided to take a $5,000 loan from his 403(b). He has to pay the loan back within five years of the date on which he received the money. He will need to pay back the initial amount, plus a pre-determined sum of interest. Mark bought the ring and gave it to Jason.

Now, it's three years later. Mark has not paid back his 403(b) for any of the loan, but he's decided to work on that over the next two years. Mark and Jason did get married, and they are living happily—when Jason is offered a promotion in another state. Mark decides to move with him and resign from Dollyville High School. He is able to get a job rather quickly in the new state. So, how much is the true cost of Jason's ring?

You might assume that it's $5,000 plus the interest that was added to the loan. In this case, that's incorrect. When you borrow from a 403(b), the interest you are charged is put back into your actual account—you don't lose that money. What you have lost is time. As we've seen, time is more valuable than money. Mark lost a few years of compounding the $5,000. But in this case, he lost even more.

When Mark borrowed the money, he had five years to pay it back. But then, he switched jobs. Anyone that leaves their current employer with an outstanding loan against their 403(b) must immediately pay the money back. The employer will set the term of the repayment, but it can be as soon as a few days after you are no longer employed. It doesn't matter why you leave the job. You could resign, or be laid off, or even fired. It doesn't matter. When you leave your employer, the loan is due.

Mark didn't have the funds to pay back his 403(b) loan. Because he is younger than 59.5, he is assessed a tax penalty of 10%. In addition, the IRS now sees this $5,000 as income and Mark must pay ordinary income tax on that amount. In all, Mark owes the IRS $1,300. The true cost of the ring is all the money that the original $5,000 could have made in the 403(b) plus the amount that the $1,300 penalty could have made in the same account. Mark had 33 years left to retirement when he took out the $5,000, and twenty-nine years left when he paid the penalty. By doing some math, we can determine that the ring's true cost is $55,875.23. I hope the marriage works out.

Roger's Timeshare

Roger is a band director from North Dakota. He's single, he loves being single, and the thought of changing that does not appeal to him. He's in his twentieth year of teaching. His retirement is fully funded; however, he still has $178,000 left on a mortgage and two years left of paying $423 each month for his car.

Roger hasn't traveled much, but this past spring break he spent a week on a beach in Florida. He loved it. It was the most relaxed and happy he'd been in years. On the day before he was to return to North Dakota, Roger attended a timeshare presentation in exchange for $150 dollars off his resort bill. Initially, he only went to the presentation to get the money.

However, the salesperson made a strong case. Roger knew that he was paying $2,500 for his week at the luxury resort. The salesperson pointed out that if Roger wanted to spend a week in Florida for the next fifty years, until he was ninety-two-years-old, Roger would spend $125,000—and that was without inflation. The timeshare would only cost $35,120, plus a $924 annual maintenance fee. This would give him a week at the resort during spring every year. And if he were to die, Roger could pass the timeshare on to whomever he wants. Roger thought this was a great deal. He loved the idea of having a place to relax each year. He arranged to take the money from his savings account and signed on the dotted line. What is the true cost of the timeshare?

Timeshare presentations are a tricky thing. The problem is that the salesperson gets two hours to tell you everything positive about buying into the timeshare. However, if you were then forced to sit with me for two hours, you might come away with a different perspective.

Timeshare salespeople love to scare you with math. They take the cost of your current vacation and multiply it by a number that gets you close to death. When you compare that number to the base cost of the timeshare, the timeshare always looks really good. However, the problem with their math is that they don't take compounding into account. If you don't buy the timeshare, you can invest that money and watch it grow. Let's do some math.

First, what will the timeshare actually cost Roger if he keeps it for fifty years? It will cost the initial $35,120, plus $924 each year. Although, is Roger really supposed to believe that the maintenance fee is never going to increase? To be safe, we'll assume that the average maintenance fee during the next fifty years is $1,124. Since timeshares are a real estate transaction, there are closing costs involved. Roger's closing costs are $1,880.

There is another cost that we have to discover—a hidden cost. Roger can't teleport from North Dakota to Florida. In order to use this purchase, he will need a round-trip airline ticket each year. I checked a few websites and found that the average ticket from Fargo to Tampa, in March, is $567. But since Roger will retire in twenty years, we'll only charge him for twenty years of flying. Perhaps he'll drive after retirement. The true cost of the timeshare is the compounded initial purchase price, yearly compounded payments of $1,124, the compounded closing cost, and twenty compounded payments of $567. The true cost of the timeshare is $1,570,092.89. That's quite a vacation fund!

Financially, I don't like timeshares because their true cost is exorbitantly high. As a traveler, I don't like them because places change. I'm not sure that any wonderful resort will be just as wonderful in fifty years. Sure, you can usually swap places, but that will come with a fee. I like the freedom of being able to make choices and change my mind.

My advice to Roger would have been to take the $150 presentation incentive and run. Then, back in North Dakota, he could pay off his car loan with money from his savings. He could then take $10,000 out of his savings account and put it in a money market fund. This would be his vacation account. Since he'll use the money in less than five years, it should stay in the safety of the money market. He can use $2,500 from his vacation account each year and replenish it from savings.

Georgia's Shopping Trip

Georgia, a teacher from Minneapolis, is going shopping at the Mall of America. She's been a bit depressed lately and read in a magazine that doing some "retail therapy" is a great way to feel better. The following is a list of things that Georgia bought with the price she paid for them (including tax). In parenthesis, I've listed the amount that the price of the item would have made in an index fund for forty years.

- Phone Case: $42.99 ($643.75)
- Designer Sunglasses: $93.50 ($1,400.11)
- Earrings: $12.78 ($191.37)
- Crystal Vase: $36.83 ($551.51)
- Cashmere Scarf: $129.99 ($1,946.53)
- Total: $316.09 ($4,733.27)

I know what you're thinking: *This is ridiculous. For God's sake, let the poor woman buy some earrings!* And, you're right. It is a bit ridiculous. But sometimes pushing things to the extreme is a good way to get the point across when you're actually about to buy something you don't need.

Life is about choices. It's those choices that will lead to savings or to debt. I often hear people (especially retired people) complain that they don't have money to travel. But if Georgia had just skipped this one shopping trip, where she bought nothing that she needed, she could have taken a nice trip later in life. Just think where Georgia could travel if she skipped more shopping trips.

Ann and Carolyn's Staff Development Meeting

Ann and Carolyn are a married couple that teach in the same district. Ann teaches sixth-grade math and Carolyn is a high school English teacher. Ann has thirty-two years left until retirement, and Carolyn has twenty-eight years left to teach.

Both of them have student loans from their undergraduate degrees. They are both in the same graduate program and have one year left to finish that degree. They have taken loans to pay for graduate school as well.

Ann is contributing to the district's 403(b). She doesn't know what it's invested in. Carolyn believes that she is contributing; however, she didn't sign the proper paperwork. Despite several emails from HR, Carolyn has not stopped by their office to complete the enrollment process.

They have a mortgage on their townhouse. While Carolyn's car is completely paid off, Ann just bought a new car with a six-year loan. They both have consumer debt on various credit cards.

Each Friday, a group of their colleagues gets together at a bar in the next town. They call this their "Staff Development Meeting." Ann and Carolyn attend this meeting, on average, three out of four weeks. When they attend, they each have two drinks that cost seven dollars each. What is the true cost of their staff development meeting?

Let's look at the numbers first. There are around thirty-six school weeks each year. (This accounts for summer, spring break, and holiday break.) Ann and Carolyn will drink with their colleagues in twenty-seven of these weeks. They spend $28 each time. This is $758 each year.

Ann has thirty-two years until retirement. Carolyn has twenty-eight years left. But Ann will probably still attend with Carolyn, even after she has already retired. The cost of the drinks is

$89,393.53. This amount is compounded, but it's not the true cost—not yet. There is also tax and tips to consider. Sales tax, plus an additional alcohol tax, is 8.5% in the town where they drink. They tip $1 for each drink. The true cost of the staff development hour, with tax and tips, is $109,472.88.

I know ... I know ... I know *exactly* what you're thinking. *They work hard. They should be able to go out and enjoy life with their co-workers. Nobody wants to work with people who never socialize.* You're right. Ann and Carolyn should be able to hang out with their colleagues. But they can't—and it's their own fault. They have made terrible choices with their money. The fact that Carolyn hasn't completed her 403(b) paperwork is enough to prohibit spending money on alcohol, let alone all the other bad choices they've made.

Alcohol served in bars and restaurants is extremely over-priced. But that doesn't mean you should never order it. If you are a grown-up, have no debt, and have fully funded your retirement, then you can drink. If not, then you can't. Could they continue to go to staff development and order a Diet Coke? No! They can't afford that either. This couple needs to seriously consider the difference between a want and a need.

Giorgio's Move

Giorgio is in his fourteenth year of teaching. He has his master's degree and has contributed the maximum allowed to his 403(b) since his first day on the job. He has a mortgage and a car loan—neither are extravagant. He has no student loans.

Two years ago, Giorgio and his wife had an amicable divorce. They have two kids together, who are both in junior high. The kids live primarily at their mother's, but Giorgio lives less than a mile away. He supports the kids financially and sees them often, mostly because they attend the school where he teaches.

However, Giorgio's ex-wife received a nice promotion. The promotion comes with a sizable raise but will require a move 125 miles away. Because the raise is too good to pass up, she plans to take the job and move with the kids. Giorgio wants to move as well and continue to be close to his kids.

In his current district, Giorgio is on the pay scale at step fourteen of twenty-five. He has already been offered a teaching job at the new school where his kids will attend after they move. In this new district, the pay scale only has eight steps. In their offer letter to him, Giorgio learned that he will be placed on step four of this district's pay scale. He will lose $6,340 in salary. Other than that, the new district offers a similar benefits and retirement package. What is the true cost of moving?

This is an easy one—no calculator required. The real question in this scenario is: What is the true cost of *not* moving? Amicable divorces are rare. These kids have two parents who want to be near them and involved in their lives. Giorgio must make this happen. This is a need and not a want.

However, he should be careful not to use the need to make excuses for a want. People do this—a lot—and it causes great financial harm. Giorgio needs to move near his kids. He doesn't need to buy a huge house and nicer car. Hopefully, he will avoid the trap of disguising a want as a need.

Financially speaking, Giorgio has a few things to consider. Because the new district only has eight steps on their pay scale, he will be able to climb much faster than at his previous district. This means that his reduction in salary will not last long. If we had the pay scales in front of us, we could do the exact math. But even without looking at them, I'm willing to bet that he will come out ahead. (In addition, if he didn't take the job, he'd spend a lot of money on transportation. That money will eat away at the salary discrepancy until it is, basically, a moot point.)

As far as retirement is concerned, things are looking good for Giorgio. We know that he's made good choices, so far, and that trend is likely to continue at the new district. The nice thing about a 403(b) is that it moves with you. In the olden days of traditional pensions and severances, Giorgio would have had to leave most of his retirement behind. But now he can take his 403(b) to the new district. If the new district has approved his vendor, Giorgio may even be able to keep the same shopping cart. If not, he will need to start the process of shopping at the grocery store over again. But don't worry, it will not harm him to have more than one shopping cart. Remember, $100 that earns 7% is $107, whether it's all in one cart or split between two. (And, this is a great way to diversify.)

Giorgio will need to do a little work when it comes to his Teacher Retirement System. If his new district is in the same TRS as his previous district, then Giorgio has absolutely nothing to do. As far as the TRS is concerned, Giorgio never moved. He will keep the same account and continue to work toward their pre-determined retirement age.

If Giorgio moves to a different state, or if he moves from a large city that had its own TRS, then Giorgio will have to switch to a new TRS. When this happens, he will start in the new system at zero: zero years of service and zero payroll contributions. He won't have a choice in this regard. But he will have a choice as to what should be done with the money in his previous TRS.

There are two options. Giorgio can take a pay-out from his previous TRS, or he can leave the money in its current account. If he takes the pay-out, he will be given a lump sum of his employee contributions. Depending upon the TRS, he may get some of the interest earned from that money and, perhaps, some of his employer contribution. Each TRS has its own rules about people who leave their system. What can Giorgio do with this lump sum? Well—anything he wants. He could buy a car, or make a down payment on a house, or even go on vacation. Although, if he does any of these things, he is making a huge mistake. He needs to save whatever lump sum he gets and put it toward retirement.

Giorgio may decide to leave the TRS money to sit. In this case, that account will continue to grow in interest, but he will not be able to contribute any new money. He will also not earn any additional years of service. But at some point, he will reach the TRS retirement age and begin collecting a monthly check until he dies. He will also get a monthly check from his new TRS. Each check will be smaller, but together they *may* add up to a normal TRS amount.

How will Giorgio decide what to do with his TRS? There is only one way to make an informed decision—he must hire a CFP®. A CFP, after being hired with a one-time fee, will gather detailed information about Giorgio and his TRS accounts. The CFP will use advanced financial math to predict the outcome of both options. There are many variables that will need to be considered—this is why Giorgio must hire a professional. Everything from Giorgio's health history to the stability of the TRS accounts will need to be analyzed mathematically. The CFP will give a recommendation to Giorgio.

In the end, Giorgio must make the move because being close to his kids is an absolute need. As long as he stays smart with his retirement, and doesn't squander any money he's already earned, he will be able to be secure financially and paternally.

Joan's Grandma

Joan's grandma gave her some great advice, and Joan was smart enough to follow it. Joan is a middle school science teacher in Oklahoma. Her grandma told her to set aside $5,000 every year, on top of retirement savings, just to be safe. Joan opened a Roth IRA and invested the money in an index fund. She plans to do this each year until she retires at the age of sixty-five. How much will her special "grandma" fund be worth on her retirement day?

This one is easy to figure out; however, we are missing the most crucial piece of information: How old is Joan when she makes her first deposit? I omitted that intentionally.

Most of the scenarios in this assignment tended to focus on people rather early in their teaching careers. I did this so that you could see the awesome power of compounding. But you can start saving at any time. In fact, there will never be another day as good to start as today. Tomorrow will never be worth as much. This means that no matter your age or teaching experience, there will never be a better time to start saving than right now.

For your information, I've listed the amount that Joan's "grandma" fund will be worth on her retirement day, listed according to her age when she first began to contribute.

35	$546,090.77
40	$367,419.12
45	$240,028.70
50	$149,201.09
55	$84,442.26
60	$38,270.11
61	$30,766.45
62	$23,753.70
63	$17,199.72
64	$11,074.50
65	$5,000

Yes, if Joan starts when she's thirty-five-years-old she will have more than half a million dollars by listening to her grandma. But look at the numbers—if she doesn't start until she's sixty, she'll still have a nice chunk of money that would buy groceries for a long time.

Life Is About Choices and Priorities

There is no doubt in my mind that the people in each of these scenarios would be happier if they'd made a financially prudent decision. I don't have a doubt, because I know what they'd choose if they were able to make the decision in reverse. At sixty-five-years old, if I asked Jake to choose between a new SUV and a check for $214,420.32, I know he'd choose the check. If I asked Jane to choose between coffee and $210,724.26, I know she'd choose the money.

I realize that these last two assignments (on debt and saving) haven't been fun at all. I'm not writing about it to be negative or to annoy you until you stop spending money. I'm writing it because there is one thing that keeps me up at night. I count many teachers among my friends and family. It scares the hell out of me when I think of any of them teaching at the age of seventy-five. I don't want that for anyone I love. And, frankly, it's not good for the students, either.

Remember, the more you save, the more you will find happiness in saving. Start today, and tomorrow will be easier.

Second Recess Break: *A Hallmark Christmas Movie—The Sequel*

Theme parks are number five on my list of loves. The complete list is my husband, then narwhals, then Christmas, then Dolly Parton, and finally, theme parks. (Going to Dollywood with my husband at Christmas is my idea of heaven—especially if I'm wearing my narwhal Christmas sweater!)

I'm not even Christian and I love Christmas—I always have. There is just something so wonderful about the decorations, the special food, and the sense that magic is real. I'm one of those people who starts to deck the halls on November 1. I'm not happy until it looks like Mrs. Claus has thrown up all over our living room. (Be advised: Christmas can get a lot of people into financial trouble. Like everything else, understand the true cost of each gift and every piece of gingerbread.)

Every year, one of the highlights of the season is the movies on the Hallmark Channel. Hallmark Christmas movies take place in my ideal world. Everyone is good-looking. The holiday decorations are perfect and the music always in tune. The good people get rewarded at the end and the bad people get what's coming to them. When it snows, it only snows just enough to be beautiful and not so much that it ruins your plans. Also, when it snows, it's still warm enough that you only need a stylish light jacket. But the most wonderful part of this world is that everyone has plenty of money—unless they have chosen to live rustically because they have plenty of money in the bank. (Seriously, have you seen the houses these Hallmark Christmas characters live in?)

These movies are comforting to me. Even though they make thirty films each year with pretty much the same plot, I watch them all. I like believing, if only for ninety minutes (without commercials), that this world is real. However, at some point I have to realize that the pristine world of Hallmark isn't real. That's when I wonder what happens next.

A Hallmark Christmas Movie

When we first met Brittany, she was a highly successful corporate attorney in New York City. She is so successful, in fact, that she's up for partner. Even though her neighbors are cranky and nobody is nice to her on the street, she's living the life that she always wanted. Brittany's fiancée, Richard Charlton III, is a guy who works on Wall Street. He is handsome in that devilish sort of way. He's nice to Brittany, but also somewhat elusive. (Clearly, since he wears a suit and works on Wall Street, there is something really bad about him.)

In order for Brittany to get her promotion to partner, she must prove herself by organizing a gingerbread bake-off in the small town of Beautiful Welcoming Valley, Vermont. Everything is riding on her ability to pull off the perfect gingerbread bake-off. (It's never fully explained what a corporate law firm in New York has to do with a small-town baking contest.)

Brittany, quite reluctant and stressed, arrives in Beautiful Welcoming Valley to discover that there isn't even a decent coffee shop in the town. Plus, nobody locks their doors and the innkeeper's wife is way too friendly. Brittany stomps down the street, attempting to find a restaurant that doesn't serve carbs, when she is run over by a bicyclist. She's fine. The bike is driven by a seemingly rude man who is pretty much the hottest person to ever walk on the planet. Seriously, this guy is so smoking hot that he can make your teeth sweat. Brittany shouts at him and stomps away.

Later, when Brittany is inspecting the venue for the baking contest, the roof suddenly collapses on her. She's fine. But the only man who can fix the roof in time for the contest is the hot guy from the bicycle accident! His name is Tucker. He's a single father with a charming six-year-old girl. His wife died of cancer. He hasn't been on a date since she passed, even though he's pretty much the hottest person who ever walked on the planet.

They bicker a lot over mundane things. Then Tucker explains that everyone in the town works for the Puppy Baby Christmas Tree Factory—and, an evil corporation in New York is trying to shut down the factory! They bond over the town's struggle to keep the factory open. Brittany starts to have real feelings for Tucker and goes on a date with him. (It's okay for her to cheat on her fiancée because he lives in the city and works on Wall Street.)

Suddenly, the evil corporation sends a man to close the Puppy Baby Christmas Tree Factory. It's Richard Charlton III! Brittany must now choose between Richard Charlton III and Christmas. Fortunately, we discover that Tucker went to college with Richard's boss. Tucker uses that connection, plus the town's Christmas spirit, to convince the corporation to spin off the factory so that it will be employee-owned.

Brittany finally realizes that Richard Charlton III is no good for her because he hates Christmas and probably eats babies. She sends him packing. Brittany understands that life in Beautiful Welcoming Valley is so much better than life in New York City. Plus, it doesn't hurt that the man she ends up with, Tucker, is pretty much the hottest person to ever walk on the earth. Brittany and Tucker kiss under the mistletoe in the softly falling snow. Even though it's cold enough to snow, we still can't see their breath—that's the true magic of Christmas.

A Hallmark Christmas Movie—The Sequel

Brittany looked into Tucker's beautiful eyes. She briefly glanced through the softy falling snow and saw Richard Charlton III slink silently back to New York. For the first time in a very long while, she was happy.

"Merry Christmas, you two!" shouted a voice from down the street. Brittany and Tucker pulled apart to see the innkeeper's wife skipping toward them.

"I'm so happy for you," said the woman when she approached.

"Thank you," Brittany replied, "and a very merry Christmas to you, too!"

"Everything is magical tonight, isn't it?" the woman asked. "Oh, by the way ... Brittany, your law firm called. Because you quit in order to start your own practice in Beautiful Welcoming Valley, they aren't going to pay your hotel bill. So, you owe me $4,842.82. I'll just charge your credit card. Anyway, have a wonderful new year!"

Brittany watched the woman bounce away up the street. It was starting to snow harder now, and she noticed that Tucker's gorgeous hair was collecting a fair amount of sparkling frozen water.

"Do you have $4,842.82 that I could borrow?" she asked Tucker.

"No—I'm a single father. Remember?" he replied. "You're a bigshot lawyer. You must have lots of money."

"Not really. Have you seen how many outfits I've worn in the past ninety minutes? The shoes alone are more than my entire salary."

"Well, I don't have any money. I'm a handyman in a very small town. I only made two chickens and a box of Russell Stover chocolates during the entire last month. You don't want to know what I have to do to make ends meet. Let's just put it like this ... the innkeeper's wife isn't happy only because it's Christmas."

Brittany replied, "Hey! I don't want to hear that kind of innuendo. Take that stuff over to Lifetime."

Just then, a group of angry senior citizens came pouring out of the Duck Lodge. They stomped out into the street, saw Brittany, and pushed themselves in a riotous fury over to her.

"What the hell are you trying to do to us?" shouted one angry man in the front.

"What do you mean? We've saved your jobs and the town," said Tucker. "We've saved Christmas!"

"No, you've ruined us," the man shouted back. "That Richard guy came and told us that he had it all worked out with headquarters in New York. Yes, they were closing the factory. But each of us was going to get a severance equal to four years of salary. Plus, those of us close to retirement were going to get to keep our pension. Now that the factory is employee-owned, we are getting nothing except the chance to wake up early tomorrow and get to work!"

"Yeah, he's right," screamed an angry woman. "I was looking at a sweet pension and now I find out that I don't even have health insurance because New York cut us off already."

"What?" Brittany asked. "You mean that Richard Charlton III negotiated for you to get all that?"

"Of course," said the man. "What did you think? That everyone on Wall Street is evil and would cut people off at Christmas? They don't want that publicity. Richard is a good man, but by now he's back in New York and having dinner in a decent restaurant."

The weather was suddenly an all-out blizzard. The shops along the street were disappearing in a sheet of white.

"I'm sorry that this has happened," Brittany said. "I'm not sure what we can do about it. Why don't we all go to dinner and sing some Christmas carols? That will make everything better."

"Oh, sorry," said Tucker. "I don't have any money to go to dinner."

Brittany stood in the blizzard and began to contemplate her life. She didn't know if she'd made a mistake. But she did know that she was hungry and had no financial plan to fall back on.

"Oh, wait!" Tucker shouted suddenly. "I just remembered that I'm the prince of a very small country in Europe that you've never heard of. Let's get on my private plane and fly away into the night. And because of the time change, we can still make it to the palace for Christmas!"

"Oh, Tucker," Brittany said with joyful tears forming in her eyes, "you are the best Christmas gift I've ever received. Merry Christmas, my sweet prince."

So, with the town watching, Brittany and Prince Tucker ran off in the direction of his plane. And they lived happily ever after. Except for the factory workers, who still lost their pensions and healthcare. And except for Tucker's daughter, who wasn't mentioned in the sequel.

THE END

Assignment Number Seven: ***Protect Your Ass-ets***

Insurance, as I've said before, is a necessary evil of life. It's one of those things that you spend a lot of money on and hope that you never need it. But that's that whole point—you hope that you don't need it. You can't ever know that you won't need it. Because of that uncertainty you must have the necessary insurances to protect your assets.

Insurance should be looked at as a protection mechanism. It should not normally be considered an investment. There are a few situations in which a variable annuity might make sense, but most of us should stay away from insurance-based investments.

Without insurance, you can lose everything you've ever worked for in a moment. Just think about what it would feel like to reach retirement age and then lose every cent you have to something that wasn't your fault. You could lose your home, your cars, and your ability to support yourself.

Homeowner's, Renter's, and Automobile Insurance

These are the three insurances that we all know about. In some cases, you are legally required to hold them. But even if you're not, you must always be covered. I don't worry all that much about losing my possessions, or even a car. Yes, that would hurt, but it wouldn't destroy my finances. However, I do worry about people litigating against me if they should get hurt in my home or car. That amount of money could absolutely ruin my financial future.

Don't be afraid to shop around for these insurances. Also, don't go crazy with the coverage amounts. Because accidents are rare, it might be in your best interest to go for a higher deductible.

You can save money by bundling—buying all your insurances from the same company. You should also ask what kind of discounts you can receive. You might be able to get a discount just by being a teacher! However, if a salesperson stops by your classroom, it's probably better to pass. Do your own research on your own terms.

Life Insurance

There are two main types of life insurance: whole and term. Whole life insurance is more of an investment and is not something that most people need. That's all I'm going to say about it because this is all the space it deserves.

However, you might need term life insurance. With term life insurance, you will pay a monthly premium for a set period of time. If you should die during that time, your beneficiary will get the death benefit of the policy. The more you pay for the premium, the higher the death benefit. If you don't die during the set amount of time, then the policy runs out and you go on your merry way. (Yes, if you live through the term, you won't get any money back. But the benefit of not getting any money back is that you're alive.)

You need term life insurance if someone else, or a bunch of someone elses, are dependent upon your income. Single people, in most cases, do not need term life insurance. Married people need it if one of the spouses can't afford to live if the other one dies. (Take the policy out in the name of the person who makes more. If both spouses are dependent upon each other, they both need term life insurance.) Families with children need to consider the paychecks of each parent. If the family can't live without both paychecks, then both parents need term life insurance.

You only need coverage until the dependent party, or parties, is able to care for themselves. Parents need to have coverage until their youngest child is around twenty-five years old. Don't pay for a longer term than you need. Couples will need term life insurance until they reach retirement age. At that point, no salary is coming in, and nothing will need to be replaced should someone die.

How much coverage should you get? A good place to start is twelve times the salary of the person whom you are insuring. By using and investing that money, the survivors should have around fifteen years to get back on their feet.

Health Insurance

My mom graduated from college on Friday, got married on Saturday, and started her first day of teaching on Monday. My grandpa used to joke that she had cost him a day's pay. Her coverage on his health insurance plan ended at 11:59 p.m. on the day she got married. However, her district's health insurance policy wouldn't begin until 12:00 a.m. on Monday. She would have one day, Sunday, without health insurance. My grandpa had to take out a separate health insurance policy for her that only lasted one day. Was this really necessary? Absolutely!

You can debate the politics and fairness of it as much as you want, but it won't change that fact that in the United States, one hospital visit can ruin your savings. What if her appendix or gall bladder had ruptured on that Sunday? What if she'd severely cut herself? Worse, what if that Sunday was the day she was diagnosed with cancer? If you live in the U.S., then you must have health insurance every single day.

As a teacher, you and your family are most likely covered by a traditional insurance plan, a health savings plan, or some combination of the two. You are also most likely paying for a portion of your health premiums through your paycheck.

Any lapses in coverage you may experience will be due to some sort of life change. Marriages, divorces, job changes, births, and deaths are examples of life changes that may trigger a lapse in coverage. When your life changes, be aware of your health insurance and make sure you are covered.

As you approach retirement, you'll need to investigate the most financially sound way to get the coverage you will need as you age. Your district, through the contract negotiation process, may cover part of your premiums from when you retire until you reach the age of Medicare. (However, as retirement ages continue to rise, this may become a moot point.) In most cases, your district must allow you to stay as part of the group, with the benefit of lower premiums, until you are eligible for Medicare.

Let's say you are retired, continuing on your school district's group plan, and still a few years away from Medicare. Could your former colleagues negotiate away your health benefits? Could they do this even though you don't have a voice at the table? Yes! Unfortunately, in most cases, retirees are not guaranteed to keep the benefits included in the last contract they worked under. The current teachers' negotiators can trade retiree healthcare for higher wages for younger teachers. As a retiree, you must always stay in contact with your former colleagues so that you are informed of any proposed changes to your benefits.

Even when you do reach the age of Medicare, you might want to purchase a supplement. Supplements are plans that you pay for on your own. They will provide specific coverage that exceeds what Medicare normally covers. These supplement plans are likely to change as Medicare is altered over the years. When your time comes, do your research.

Long-Term Care Insurance

The purpose of insurance is to protect what you have. With that said, I'm amazed at the sheer number of people I meet who don't have long-term care insurance. They all realize the importance of home, auto, and health insurance. I don't understand why they don't see that they are one accident away from losing everything to a nursing home.

According to AARP, a person the age of sixty-five has a 50 percent chance of requiring care in a long-term facility. As you age, that chance grows. Also, according to AARP, the average annual cost of long-term care in the United States is $140,000. The cheapest state is Texas, and the most expensive is Connecticut—the rest fall somewhere in between. Imagine how you'd feel if you worked as hard as teachers do for forty years, only to see it all go to a nursing home administrator.

But don't think that nursing homes are just for old people. You might get severely injured in some sort of accident. Perhaps you only need long-term care for three months. That will still cost $11,660. Health insurance policies vary on the amount of long-term care they cover. You could be on the hook for the entire amount.

Long-term care insurance is also not just for nursing homes. Most policies cover in-home long-term assistance. They also may cover transportation costs to daily physical therapy or for special equipment that you will need in your home.

Like with other insurances, you will pay a monthly premium for long-term care. The premium will depend upon your age and amount of coverage you choose. The younger you are, the cheaper your premium will be—but you will have to pay it for longer. (Don't let it accidentally lapse!) You will need to choose your level of coverage. Coverage is based upon the daily amount that your plan will pay for your long-term care. The higher the amount you choose, the higher your premium will be. It's a good idea to go online and find out the charge for one day in a private room at a facility near your hometown. This amount can change dramatically depending upon your location.

Umbrella Insurance

Umbrella insurance, also known as excess liability insurance, is not as common as the others I've mentioned. But this extra insurance policy is quite necessary if you've learned a lot from this book.

Let's say that you have an automobile insurance policy from the Narwhal Insurance Company. You're driving down the road and, unfortunately, you get into a really bad accident. You are okay, but Mr. Smith, a passenger in another car, is seriously injured. For whatever reason, it's determined that the accident was your fault. Mr. Smith will file a claim against your insurance policy. Narwhal Insurance will settle that claim up to the maximum amount that your claim allows (usually around $1 million).

Now, Mr. Smith could also sue you for a lot more—especially if he feels his injuries warrant a higher amount. But since you don't have much money, Mr. Smith isn't going to go through all the trouble, and expense, of taking you to court.

However, let's now say that you followed all the advice in the book and have amassed an investment fund that's worth more than $1 million. (Don't laugh—it's more likely than you might believe. Just do the math and compound what you spent on things you didn't need during the last year.) Anyway, now Mr. Smith has an incentive to bring you to court because you do have more money.

Sure, the accident may have been your fault. But should you lose everything you've worked for? After all, it was still an *accident*. This is where umbrella insurance will protect your retirement.

If you have more than $1 million in assets, you need umbrella insurance. You can get it from your automobile insurer, and it's normally attached to that policy. Umbrella insurance is also available for your home, and if you bundle your insurance you can save money in this regard. The premiums for this type of insurance are surprisingly low. But, since this is coverage for extra assets, make sure you have the extra assets to cover before you waste the premiums.

Travel Insurance

This insurance is for those who have their futures financially secured. My husband and I are avid international travelers. We never leave the country without adequate travel insurance. However, there is a lot of misunderstanding about travel insurance and the need for it.

I meet many other travelers who tell me, "I'm covered by my credit card, so I don't need travel insurance." I've heard other travelers say, "This trip doesn't cost that much, so we decided that travel insurance would be a waste of money." Both of these statements can end up costing a lot of money.

Some credit cards do offer travel insurance as a perk of using their card to book travel. These companies love to promote this aspect of their cards. But you need to remember that seeing the words "travel insurance" is no guarantee of any specific kind of coverage. Most of these types of cards provide only some sort of catastrophic coverage. They know that the chance of you having a catastrophe while traveling is low. They get a lot of publicity out of a little coverage.

These policies cover things like plane crashes, major earthquakes, and tsunamis. It's unlikely you'll ever encounter any of these situations during your travels. For most of us, we need travel insurance to cover missed connections, labor strikes, and snowstorms. Credit card travel insurance will not cover any of these common occurrences. Another item not covered by credit cards: international medical expenses.

Perhaps your trip abroad didn't cost that much, and you're not worried about losing much money if you have to cancel. That's great—but you still need medical insurance while traveling internationally. Make no mistake about it, your domestic health insurance will not cover any medical expenses incurred outside the country. There are many travelers who do not understand this fact. I will say it again. When you leave the country, all medical expenses you accumulate will need to be paid from your own pocket.

I once had a blood vessel in my eye burst while I was in Germany. It wasn't a big deal, but I needed to make sure that there wasn't anything worse going on. I also needed antibacterial eye drops to make sure I didn't get an infection. Germany, like most other industrialized countries, has a national healthcare program. Since I'm not German, I didn't have any coverage. I had to go to a German hospital. Everything turned out okay, but I wasn't able to leave until I paid my bill. When I got home, my travel insurance reimbursed me for my expenses.

My husband got a stomach virus in the Bahamas. He became dehydrated and required IV fluids. On a different trip, he had some sort of allergic reaction in Italy. These unexpected annoyances were covered by our travel insurance. The medical situations I've written about are minor (insert the sound of me knocking on wood here). However, what if one of us gets hit by a car? What if someone falls and breaks something? What if I need my appendix removed? What if my husband has an abscessed tooth? These things happen—and they can be quite expensive.

Aside from medical expenses, travel insurance will cover trip cancellation and travel delay. We had to cancel a trip to Iceland once because my mother-in-law fell and broke her hip. We shortened a trip to London because my Grandma Francy died. Again, travel insurance reimbursed our expenses so that we could be with our families and save our money to travel in the future.

Travel insurance will also cover unexpected delays and emergencies. In 2019, we were stuck north of the Arctic Circle on Baffin Island. The only plane available had mechanical issues. It's expensive to be stuck in a place with limited services. We were very happy to have had travel insurance on that trip. Can you imagine the expense if you needed to be airlifted out of a country due to a protest or war?

Don't let your entire retirement go to the French national health system because you had a heart attack in Paris. Travel insurance is not expensive, and it's easy to purchase. There are several companies that offer travel insurance online. Most of the time, your premium will be based upon the amount you paid for the trip, your age, the coverage you select, and the duration of the trip. There may be some situations where your desired destination is more expensive. You might pay more for travel insurance if you travel to a high-risk country than if you travel to Canada or Europe.

When you investigate travel insurance, you'll be presented with a few coverage options. Don't go crazy here. Look for a policy that covers the cost you paid for the trip and a moderate amount of medical coverage. If you're going somewhere remote, or a place prone to political instability, then you'll also want evacuation insurance.

When you travel, and you encounter an unfortunate situation, make sure that you keep all documents. You can't have too much documentation in this regard. When you are ready, most travel insurance companies will ask you to file a claim online. Send them everything you have including receipts, letters from travel providers, photos, and medical reports. You may also be asked to submit proof of death if you are canceling your trip because someone close to you died. I've also found it helpful to call the company as soon as you have a problem. They will record that call as proof of your claim.

Other Things That Can Bite Your Ass-ets

We've talked about insurance—something you do in order to protect your finances. Now we'll talk about a few things *not* to do. Each of these can cause serious damage to your financial future.

Co-signing Loans

The first is co-signing for a loan. When you co-sign a loan, it means that the applicant isn't able to prove to the bank that they will have the ability to pay back the loan, plus interest. The bank will only lend the money if the applicant can produce a "back-up" person to fulfill the requirements of the loan. If the original applicant, regardless of circumstances, does not make payments toward the loan, the co-signer must assume this financial responsibility. It doesn't matter why. The original applicant can stop paying simply because they don't want to, and the co-signer is on the hook for the entire amount of the loan. Plus, the co-signer has no legal right to whatever the applicant bought with the loan in the first place.

Never, ever, co-sign a loan for anyone who is not your child. Don't do it for friends, family, or your very favorite cousin. More relationships have been ruined over the co-signing of loans than anything else on this planet—just watch a daytime court television show if you doubt me. If the bank won't trust the applicant, then you shouldn't either.

You can co-sign a loan for one of your children, but only if both of the following conditions are met.

1. The loan must be required for an absolute need that will make it possible for your child to start building a financial future on their own.
2. You must have enough money to pay back the loan without any negative consequences on your own finances.

There is a possibility that one of your kids may need help to start their adult life. You might be the only person who is willing to trust them enough to put your name on a piece of paper. But this is not to be used for a new car, fancy equipment, or a trip to India to learn how to teach yoga. Only co-sign a loan for costs that are needed to begin adult life. And, always assume that you will end up making the payments. Don't risk ruining you the future of your family relationships, and the future of your finances, by co-signing for an amount you can't afford.

Addictions

All of us make mistakes. It's a part of life. Fortunately, most mistakes can be financially solved with time. Unfortunately, having an addiction is one mistake that can dig a hole so deep you may never recover financially.

I stated earlier that money isn't everything, but everything requires money. It can also be said that money can't solve all your problems, but all your problems consume money. Addictions cost a lot of money, both directly and indirectly.

You've probably already assumed that I'm talking about drug, alcohol, smoking, and gambling addictions. You're right—they consume an unbelievable amount of money. However, you can get addicted to many more things that drain your wallet.

I've known people who are addicted to quilting. Yes, it sounds funny. And, it's okay to laugh ... at least until you visit a fabric store with a financial calculator. Quilting can cost an addict thousands of dollars each year. I know people with more fabric in their homes than in New York's fashion district. There's nothing wrong with quilting for a hobby, as long as it doesn't consume more than you can afford.

I knew a woman once who had an absolute addiction to charity. She made a lot of money as a vice president of a major bank, and gave it all away. She loved seeing all the good that her money could do for people in need. She also relished in the awards she received. There's nothing wrong with giving to charity. But there is something wrong when you give everything to charity. This woman eventually was forced to claim bankruptcy. Like most addicts, she required a great amount of therapy to learn why she made these choices. Even though she has learned her lesson, it will take years before she can move past bankruptcy.

Do you have a quilting addiction? It might come in the form of porn, model airplanes, baking, nutritional supplements, gaming, or millions of other ways.

You've sacrificed a lot to become financially secure. Recognize the signs of addiction early so that you don't give your money away. Most recovered addicts admit that, very early on, they knew they were headed down the wrong path. If you find yourself on that path, seek help immediately.

Don't Lose Your Ass-ets

Insurance seems like such a waste of money. After all, most of the time, you are paying for something without seeing any benefit. Again, that's the whole point. Be grateful that you didn't see a benefit, and go on with your life.

You will work very hard to acquire the money you need to be financially secure. Don't risk losing it because something happens that's beyond your control.

Assignment Number Eight: *Maintenance Isn't Just for School Custodians*

Let's talk about custodians. My dad was a career custodian. He started cleaning office buildings at night, moved to cleaning a convent, and ended up at a public school. He never spent a cent on higher education, yet managed to make a living and retire. He's been to forty-nine states. (Due to circumstances unrelated to finances, he won't fly. You can guess which state he hasn't been to.) My dad has been on several cruises and traveled internationally.

Here's another thing about custodians: they can be quite wealthy. My husband works for the federal government. Every few years, his agency's retirement specialist makes a visit and gives presentations. We always attend when they are offered. As part of the presentation, the retirement specialist shares figures related to the state of retirement. He always talks about the TSP millionaires. A TSP millionaire is someone who has more than $1 million in their TSP account. (TSP is the federal government's version of a 403(b).)

Here's the shocking thing: The TSP millionaires are never the government's physicians or lawyers. They are always the janitors and food service workers. These are people who started working right out of high school, never paid for higher education, and contributed the maximum each year to their TSP. After learning these facts, I don't want to hear another teacher tell me that it's impossible to save for retirement. If someone who starts at minimum wage can do it, so can you.

This assignment is about maintenance. Your car needs maintenance as well as your house. Your own body needs maintenance. Your finances are no different. A financial plan is only as good as your ability to monitor and maintain it.

I don't know why I continue to be shocked at the level of indifference people have about their finances. I should have gotten over it by now. However, it's shocking to me that people don't know where their money is. I know people who can tell you the exact wines they drank on their last overpriced trip to California. But they have no idea if they own a traditional IRA or Roth IRA. Again, if this is you, there are no excuses—it's your future self that will suffer.

Like almost everything else in life, maintaining your finances gets easier each time you do it. Every single month, you must sit down with your computer and go through absolutely everything you own. Check each account and make sure the numbers reflect what you expect. Go through every credit card charge and match it up to your receipts. Take care of any discrepancy. This is the best way to avoid identity theft and to prevent against fraud.

When you are looking at your investment accounts, if something doesn't make sense, you need to find out the answer. Call a professional and ask whoever administrates the account for you. Check each metaphorical shopping cart, basket, and item.

In our modern times, there really is no excuse for not knowing where every cent is at any given moment. Every bank, discount brokerage firm, and financial service provider offers an app where you can check your finances in real time. If you ask either me or my husband where our money is, both of us can tell you the exact amounts without hesitation.

While I am mentioning my husband, I want to stress the importance of financial awareness for those who are legally married.

Both participants in a marriage must know everything about their family's finances. Women tend to have a bad reputation for not knowing what their husbands are doing financially—but I'm telling you that it's a universal problem. I know gay men who have no idea what is going on in their accounts and let their husbands take care of it. I know straight guys who rely on their wives to pay all the bills, and gay women who mindlessly hope their spouse has everything covered.

If you are married, you must sit down with each other and go through all your accounts—every single month. I know this can be quite a chore with children, teaching, and other business to manage. But both partners need to know exactly where every cent is at all times. Not only will you make better choices if you know where all your money is, but you will be better protected as well. Unfortunately, not every marriage will end up happily ever after. Hopefully yours will. But if you don't know your complete financial picture—and you split with your spouse for whatever reason—you are in for a very long road.

No matter if you are single, married, or something between, checking all your accounts is something that you must do each and every month. Trust me—it will get easier. Checking your accounts will become a fun way of noticing how smart you are.

Personal Information

Once each year, check the personal information on each of your accounts. Make sure your name is spelled correctly and that your address is current. Check that your email address is correct. Computers can make a mistake—so can people who input information. This once-per-year check will assure that the account's administration can contact you appropriately.

Beneficiaries

Also, once each year, you must check your beneficiaries. This is non-negotiable. You must do it. In the world of retirement, beneficiaries are king. They rule over marriages, wills, and even children.

That same retirement specialist for the federal government, whom I wrote about earlier, has many horror stories to tell about people who did not update their beneficiaries. He can tell you, in detail, about the many times that a wife called him, asking where her recently deceased husband's pension check was. After checking into it, he regretfully would have to tell her that the check was going to his first wife—a woman he hadn't seen in over twenty years! The husband had never changed his beneficiary and there was nothing that the current wife could do about it. There was no court that could help her. This is not an isolated example—unfortunately, it is a common occurrence.

You must also be careful with listing no beneficiary for an account. In some states, a blank beneficiary means that the assets of the account are distributed *per stirpes*. This means that the state has defined a hierarchy of people who will receive the assets in a pre-determined order. However, some states do not have a per stirpes procedure. In those states, public retirement accounts will revert back to the state! I know of a woman who fought hard to get her deceased husband's pension. He worked for a public university for over thirty years. He'd never filled out a beneficiary form despite a reminder each year that came to him in writing. But there was nothing that could be done for this woman. No court would hear the case, and all his pension money went back to the state. The final word from the judge: Without a completed beneficiary form, there was no way of knowing that he didn't *want* to keep his wife from getting his pension.

If you've been teaching for a few years, check your beneficiaries right now. Don't forget to check your Teacher Retirement System. You might be surprised. Who knows what your twenty-two-year-old self thought was a good idea? Relationships change throughout life, and your beneficiaries need to reflect that.

Your Approaching Mortality

It's so hard to think about. It can cause discomfort at best, and extreme panic attacks at worst. But it's a fact that all of us started dying the day we were born. Maintenance also involves maintaining your finances ever after you've gone to that big teachers' lounge in the sky.

Everyone, no matter how much they know about finances, needs professional help in this regard. First, it's difficult to understand the enormous complexity of the estate legal system unless you study it full-time. Second, you are too close to the situation and need someone less involved to prepare your paperwork.

There are several devices that you might need, depending upon your situation. These include wills, testaments, trusts, and directives. Considering your situation, you may also benefit from changing the title of any real estate you own. Then, there are some things that are not required, but that you might want. These are things like health care directives and funeral planning.

None of this stuff is fun. Your future self might not even know you did all this work. But that's the point. Even if you are incapacitated, these financial devices will ensure that your desires are followed.

Once each year, you must also check and maintain any advanced directives that a professional has assembled for you.

You Owe It to Yourself

All this monthly and yearly maintenance is a chore—there is no way to sugar-coat the task. It's something that you have to do that requires time and energy. It's paperwork and concentration and math. Nobody likes these chores.

If you look at it a different way, though, financial maintenance is a way of showing love for yourself. I love myself enough that I want me to be happy. I want this happiness to last until the day I die. I don't need money because I want to have it, I need it because it will ensure that my basic needs are met so that I can do things that make me happy. I want to give that gift to myself, because I really like me.

When you sit down each month, either alone or with someone else, take a deep breath and think about what you are doing for yourself. Picture your future self. Listen as the elderly version of you says, "Thank you for doing this for me. I love you."

Assignment Number Nine: *Celebrate Your Achievement*

Finally, an assignment that won't make you want to kill me!

Think about your last day of school each year. If you're a high school teacher, you might have a big celebration like commencement. But even if you don't, you still know how it feels to watch your students leave your classroom for the last time. It doesn't matter whether you liked all your students or not—it's a happy feeling to see them leave you just a little better than when they arrived.

After accomplishing all the tasks in this book, it will be time to celebrate. You might assume that I'm going to tell you to celebrate without spending any money. You probably expect me to make a contrived list of fun things you can do that don't cost anything. Well, you are very wrong.

Here's the deal: If you're debt free, and have made sensible spending decisions, fully funded your retirement, protected your assets, and continued to maintain your financial plan—then, by all means, go out and buy anything you want that you can afford. Spend your money and go on vacation. You know how to do the math. If you can afford it, upgrade to first class and stay in the hotel with the best location.

Money is no good unless you are doing something with it. Before, saving is what you needed to do with it. But now, since you are assured that you can live financially stable for the rest of your life, go and do other things with your money.

But, somehow, I have the feeling that you won't want to. After you've experienced the joy of saving, you will probably want to fly coach. There's nothing wrong with that, either.

The Negative Side of Celebrating

Ugh! Can't anything, even celebrating, come without the dark side? It's frustrating to face the negative consequences of securing financial freedom for yourself. All of us are human—those pesky human emotions always get in the way.

Many people detest the fact that my husband and I are well-off. These people are among our friends, neighbors, colleagues, and even family. Some of it is envy, although most of it is that we are a reminder of what was possible. We are from similar backgrounds, circumstances, salaries, and genetics. When these people look at us, we become a reminder of what they likely could have had if they'd sacrificed and saved as much as my husband and I have.

It's frustrating because I still feel close to a lot of these people and I want to share my life with them. But none of them ever ask about our vacations. They never want to know what book I'm working on. They don't ask about our hobbies and interests. They never ask my husband how his job is going. It's sad. It feels a bit like we've somehow found ourselves living on a different planet.

There is another group of people that equally frustrates me. If you've read this entire book and put some of the pieces together, you have figured out that in the 1970s, I grew up as a gay guy, without much money, in a small rural Minnesota town. It probably won't surprise you to learn that some people were really mean to me. I want these people to see how well I'm doing.

I know—I know, it's my own personality fault that wants me to seek this revenge. I completely own that. I have a dream that some old relative of mine sees a photo online while they sit in their trailer drinking their own pee. The photo is my husband and me having a great time at Tokyo Disneyland. I want this old relative to know that I've won.

But it wouldn't matter. If they saw that photo, they'd just say, "Well, *my* son is unemployed and behind on his child support, but at least he's not gay." I will never be able to win with any of the people who were mean to me. People who have it within themselves to be mean to kids don't have it within themselves to be enlightened later on.

You won't win any awards for being financial stable. Nobody will congratulate you or pat you on the back. That's why it's so important that you do something to celebrate. In a way, that's the whole point. You sacrificed and worked hard to give yourself the peace of mind that you are financially set for life. That's why you get to celebrate while all those other people get to stay at home and worry about their bills.

You Are Amazing

However you intend to proceed, find some way to celebrate your amazing achievement. Take a look at your colleagues the next time you have a staff development meeting. Hardly any of them are prepared for a world where retirement ages will be high, and benefits will be low. This is not an overly dramatic statement. It's a mathematical certainly.

My husband and I are the happiest people I know. A lot of that has to do with the fact that we really enjoy each other's company. But a lot of our happiness is because our stress levels are low. We know that we have enough money to live for the rest of our lives—even if we both lost our incomes today. The amount of peace that provides is outstanding. And it is something that needs to be celebrated.

Very few people have what it takes to build wealth. You have to be strong and you have to want it more than you want anything else. If you are one of those few people who succeeds, then you truly deserve to celebrate the amazing person that you are.

Conclusion

Teachers are different than other professionals. Because they work with the future in a way that no other profession does, they form a unique outlook. Perhaps that's why so many teachers make poor decisions when attempting to secure their own financial futures.

My husband has a hard time believing that I signed away my 403(b) in the teachers' lounge to a man I'd known for five minutes. He can't even comprehend how this man was allowed to access the employees of the school district in the first place. And he can't seem to get his head around the idea that someone as educated as I am would make such an important decision without consulting at least one other person.

I had to explain to him my mindset during this time. Because of my upbringing and education, I truly believed that having money was bad. This belief was reinforced in countless movies and television shows. When I walked into the teachers' lounge that day, I didn't want to throw away my money. But since I didn't think money was that important, it was easy to sign the paperwork. In a strange way, because I believed in the superiority of the Ingalls family from *Little House on the Prairie,* I was superior to those that wanted money. It's embarrassing, and downright sick, for me to think about now. However, at the time, signing away my 403(b) was almost a badge of honor that I could pin on my soul.

I also had to admit to my husband that I believed the state would always take care of me. Retirement was so far away, and I had no understanding of how the real world worked. Perhaps that's another thing that sets teachers apart: most of us have only worked in an academic setting for our entire lives. I didn't realize that the world owed me absolutely nothing, no matter how hard I worked. I hadn't faced the fact that when I reached retirement, I would be completely on my own. If I'd sat down with a calculator, I could have seen the writing on the wall. But, inside of myself, I knew there was no way I wanted to see those words of warning. It was so much easier to remain ignorant.

And that leads me to the hardest truth. I hated to admit to my husband that I was ignorant and envious. Since I wanted to be honest with him, I also had to throw "lazy" into the mix. How could an educated person like me throw away their money in the teachers' lounge? Well, they wouldn't. But an educated person who was also misdirected, too optimistic, ignorant, envious, and lazy could absolutely make that terrible decision.

Ultimately, the good news is that none of this has to be this way. As teachers, we know that the best way to learn is by correcting our own mistakes. Let's use our amazing teaching powers to correct our financial mistakes.

Among all the professions of the world, we should understand investing more than any of them. It's what we do every single day. Most teachers will never see the immediate gains of their labors. It takes years for our students to grow and use the information we gave them to live and thrive. As teachers, we are constantly giving our energy today so that the world can receive a benefit from it later on. That's investing!

But, now, the bell is ringing, and you have to get back to your students. It's time for us all to get busy living. I wrote earlier that money isn't everything, but everything requires money. I still stand by that statement. Except, there is one thing that doesn't cost anything and can lead to total financial freedom. No, it's not love—love is free, but it can end up costing you a lot without thought. And, that's what I'm talking about here—thought.

Use your brain. Don't ignore that inner voice that is telling you to grow up and take control of your finances. I know that voice is inside you, because I ignored it in myself for years. Think about what you are doing and the decisions you are making. Use your brain.

Have a great teaching career, inspire your students, and do good things with your life. Most of all, take care of your future self.

I'd like to leave you with a quote by William A. Ward, a poet who wrote for *Reader's Digest* in the mid-twentieth century. This sentiment pretty much says it all.

Before you speak, listen.

Before you write, think.

Before you spend, earn.

Before you invest, investigate.

Before you criticize, wait.

Before you pray, forgive.

Before you quit, try.

Before you retire, save.

Before you die, give.